FIND OUT ABOUT

DINOSAURS

And the Prehistoric World

First published in the USA 1986
Published by
GALLERY BOOKS
An imprint of W.H. Smith Publishers Inc.
112 Madison Avenue
New York, New York 10016

ISBN 0-8317-3377-2
Printed in Yugoslavia

FIND OUT ABOUT

DINOSAURS

And the Prehistoric World

Dougal Dixon

GALLERY BOOKS
An Imprint of W. H. Smith Publishers Inc.
112 Madison Avenue
New York City 10016

Introduction

Have you ever wondered what it would be like to live in the mysterious world of the dinosaurs? This is the dinosaur book to answer all your questions!

If you have ever wanted to ask the scientists questions such as how do they know about life in the past, what do they do if they find a good fossil, was *Tyrannosaurus* as ferocious as all the books say it was, did a meteorite really kill them all off, and any other questions that make the study of life in the past such a puzzle, then this book will answer some of your questions.

However, the scientists themselves do not know the answers to all of these questions – if they did palaeontology, the study of ancient life, would not be nearly so exciting. And so the answer to many of the queries is a great big maybe. However, scientists can tell us what are the most likely answers, and the ones that we can accept for the time being until new discoveries and theories lead us to believe something different.

Like most books which look at life before man, this volume is not just about the dinosaurs. Although the dinosaurs were the most impressive and spectacular of the fossil animals, they were really not terribly important as far as the history of life on our planet is concerned. In this book you will find out about the other creatures that existed before the dinosaurs, at the time of the dinosaurs, and long after the dinosaurs died out, as well as the plants that were growing at that time. Questions about the world and the landscapes in which they lived are also answered. These subjects are all included in the science of palaeontology.

The book is laid out chronologically – that is, it starts from the beginning of life and works through to the present. You can start at the beginning of the book and explore your way through the history of our planet, or you can dip into *Find Out About Dinosaurs And The Prehistoric World*, finding the questions that you would particularly like to ask.

Either way you should find out a lot more than you knew before.

How old is the Earth?

As far as we know, the Earth is about 4.6 billion years old. Put another way, that is 4,600 million years, or 4,600,000,000 years. Whichever way you look at it, it's a long time.

It might be easier to imagine it as a clock, ticking off a very slow hour from the beginning of the Earth to the present day (see below). On this clock there would be no life on Earth for the first 21 minutes – representing the first 1.6 billion years of the Earth's history. Then life appeared, but we don't know very much about it.

For more than half an hour, or almost 3 billion years, the only living things were soft-bodied sea creatures. Then, at about eight minutes to the hour, or 570 million years ago, we suddenly get animals with hard shells and bones. From then on, living things spread everywhere. This last 570 million year time span is divided into the Palaeozoic era, the Mesozoic era and the Cainozoic era, and these eras are divided into many more 'periods'. Different animals and plants lived in the different periods. On our clock, man did not appear until a tenth of a second before the hour was up.

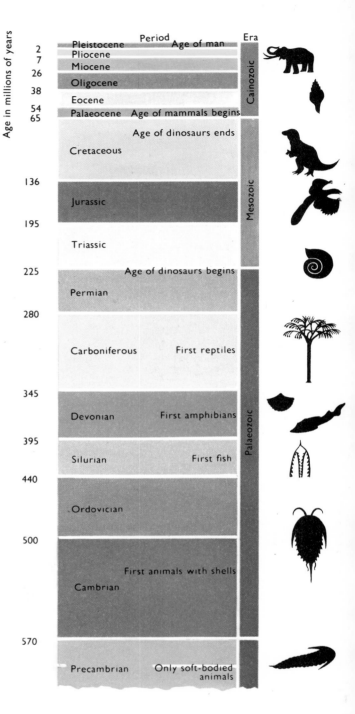

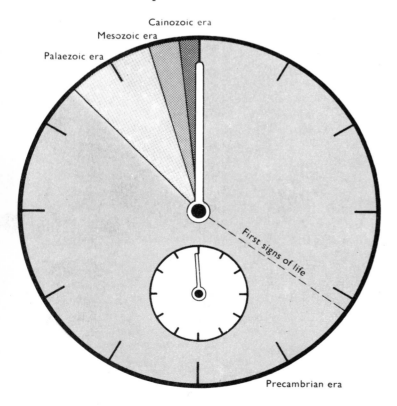

What is a geological column?

The eras and periods are usually shown as a column, starting at the bottom with the Cambrian period of the Palaeozoic era, 570 million years ago. As we read up the column we get closer to the present day. We use the names of the periods when we are talking about ancient times.

10

A cross section of the Earth's crust showing the different rock types. Sedimentary rocks are those in layers or 'beds'. The igneous rocks have pushed through them, sometimes forming volcanoes. The metamorphic rocks are the twisted ones deep down, or the discoloured areas next to the igneous masses

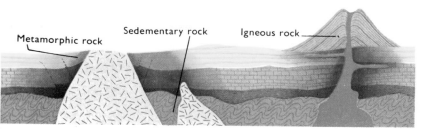

Metamorphic rock   Sedementary rock   Igneous rock

What is the Earth made of?

The Earth consists of rocks and these are formed in three different ways.

Igneous rocks form as hot molten material from inside the Earth pushes its way to the surface and cools.

Sedimentary rocks form as mud, sand or rubble piles up in layers. These layers are buried and are turned to stone.

Metamorphic rocks form when the Earth heats and crushes other rocks at great depths, and turns them into completely new types of rock.

New rocks are being formed all the time, and old ones are constantly being worn away.

Which rock is important?

We always use sedimentary rocks when we want to see what happened in the past. The different types can tell us what the land and sea were like at the time they were formed.

Shale is formed from mud, so it shows that there was a muddy swamp or sea bottom at that time. Limestone is usually made up of tiny parts of broken seashells, formed on the bottom of a shallow sea. Chalk is a fine limestone made of microscopic shells. Sandstone formed from sand in a river or desert. Coal is made of dead plants and shows that there was once a thick forest in the area. It took millions of years to turn these to stone.

Sedimentary rock is forming under this lake

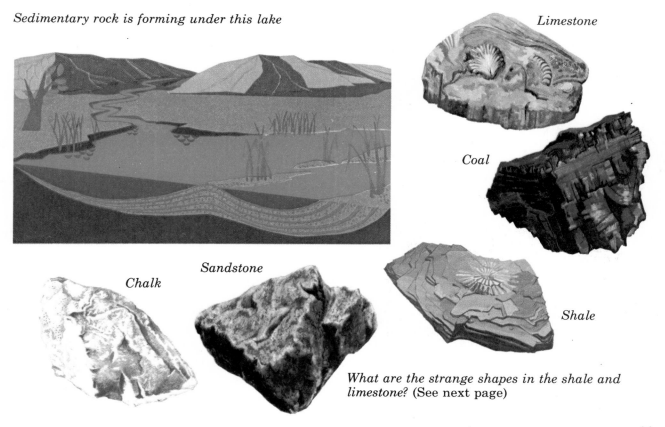

Limestone

Coal

Chalk

Sandstone

Shale

What are the strange shapes in the shale and limestone? (See next page)

What is a fossil?

When an animal or plant was embedded in a sedimentary rock millions of years ago, and we find those remains today, we call the remains 'fossils'. Some sedimentary rocks have no fossils at all. Others, such as limestone, are made up entirely of fossils.

Only a very few of the millions and millions of living things that have ever existed have become fossils. There are many different ways in which a dead animal or plant can become fossilized.

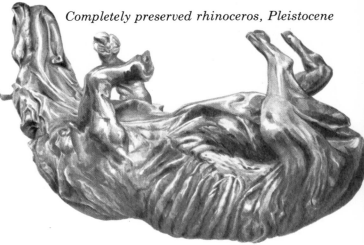

Completely preserved rhinoceros, Pleistocene

How much of the creature remains?

Sometimes the whole animal is preserved. This is very rare. The rhinoceros (above) was preserved in a natural pickling mixture of brine and tar. It is 10,000 years old and was found in Poland. We sometimes find mammoths preserved in frozen mud.

Entire insects are sometimes preserved in a mineral called amber. This formed as resin seeped from a tree and trapped an insect as it alighted on it. When the tree was eventually buried the resin turned to amber. Fossils like these tend to be quite recent – not older than a few million years.

More often, only part of the original plant or animal is left. The shark teeth (below) are harder than the rest of the shark skeleton and remain behind on the sea bed after the rest has rotted away.

During the Pleistocene, oil seeped from the ground in California and formed ponds of tar. Animals were trapped in the tar and died. Although their flesh decayed, their bones stayed embedded in the tar and can still be seen there.

Unaltered sharks' teeth, Miocene

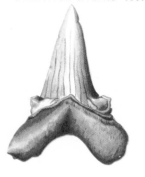

How do fossils form?

To become a fossil the body of an animal must be buried immediately, before it rots away or is eaten by something else. That is why the best fossils are made from water-living things, such as fish (above left), or from animals that live near the banks of a river. The horse (above right) has fallen into the water and is buried by the river sands.

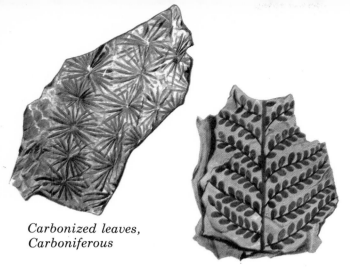

Carbonized leaves, Carboniferous

What happens to the remains?

Usually the plant or animal rots away completely and no fossil is left. Sometimes, however, only part of the substance decays, leaving something behind.

A plant is made up of the elements carbon, hydrogen and oxygen. When a plant is buried the hydrogen and the oxygen may be lost, leaving the original carbon behind in the shape of the plant.

The ferns (above) are preserved in shale from the Carboniferous period as thin films of carbon. When this happens to huge masses of vegetation, such as a forest or a lush swamp, so much carbon builds up that it forms thick beds. This is how coal is formed.

Petrified wood, Eocene

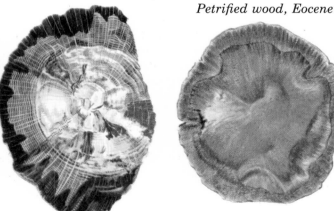

What is petrifaction?

When the carbon, hydrogen and oxygen of a buried plant are replaced by totally new elements, the result is petrified wood (above). A mineral in the surrounding sediments, such as silica, can take the place of the original material. The plant's internal shapes and structures are now made of silica.

What are a cast and a mould?

Imagine the remains of a buried creature rotting away after the mud or sand has turned to rock. That would leave a hole in the rock in the exact shape of the creature. This hole is called a mould.

Later on, when water seeps through the rock, any mineral that is dissolved in it may be deposited in the hole. This will give a mineral mass in the same shape as the hole. A fossil formed like this is called a cast.

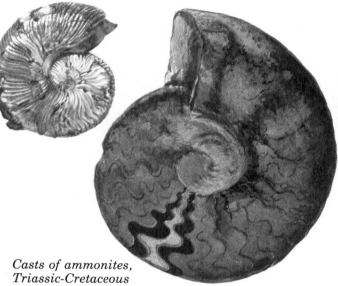

Casts of ammonites, Triassic-Cretaceous

When a cast shows the pattern of the inside of a shell (right) it is called an internal cast.

Must a fossil show the creature?

A fossil could be just the marks that an animal has left behind. Reptile footprints (below) may be preserved in sandstone, showing where an animal has walked through a desert or across a sandbank. Worm burrows in shales are quite common. This kind of fossil is called a trace fossil. It can often be very difficult to work out what kind of creature made it.

All of these fossil types can help to tell us what life was like in the past.

Reptile footprint, Triassic

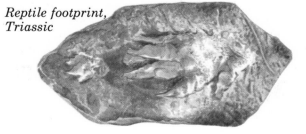

Who studies fossils?

Anybody can take up fossil collecting as a fascinating hobby. Scientists who do so, and study the life of the past, are called palaeontologists.

Their work is divided into two parts – field work and laboratory work. Field work consists of going to the places where they think the fossils they are looking for might be found. This can take months of preparation, since it may involve expeditions to the wild corners of foreign countries. They know the kinds of rocks and the types of places where they might find the fossils.

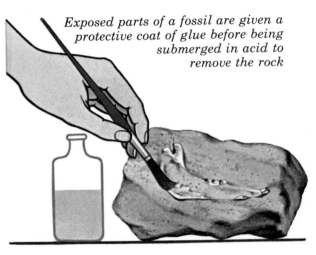

Exposed parts of a fossil are given a protective coat of glue before being submerged in acid to remove the rock

Palaeontologists look at sedimentary rocks where they appear at the surface of the Earth. They look where there have been recent rockfalls from cliffs, or where streams have cut into the rock itself. In these places the sedimentary rock will be broken open so palaeontologists can see what is inside.

A fossil is found

The palaeontologist carefully removes it from the rock

takes notes

wraps it carefully

numbers the specimen

When an interesting fossil is found in a rock, the palaeontologist removes it very carefully. He or she gives it a number and writes all the details about where and how it was found in a field notebook. The palaeontologist then packs the fossil securely, in this instance with newspaper, so that it is not damaged by bumping against other specimens in the bag on the way home

When they find something interesting, they photograph it, make notes about where it was found, remove it carefully from the rock, package it up securely and transport it back to the laboratory where they examine it.

Some fossils can be quite sturdy and can be carried quite safely wrapped in newspaper, but most are extremely delicate and must be well protected, encased in plaster of Paris.

What happens in the laboratory?

Back at the laboratory the palaeontologists remove the fossil from its packing. It must now be cleaned up so that it can be studied properly. The palaeontologists may do this or, if the laboratory is in a museum or a university, this work may be done by technicians who have been specially trained to handle the delicate specimens.

Sometimes the fossil is removed from the rock using dentists' drills, small chisels or other tools. Often the palaeontologist or technician coats the fossil with a kind of glue to protect it while the pieces of sedimentary rock are chipped away.

Another method is to use acid. This works well if the fossil is petrified or is a cast in an acid-resistant mineral such as silica (see page 13) and is embedded in limestone. The specimen is kept in acid for several hours at a time and then washed thoroughly and inspected.

Any loose rock is washed off, the newly exposed parts of the fossil are protected with a coat of glue, and then it is put back into the acid for another treatment. This continues until the whole fossil is visible.

All these methods take a long time, and it is very delicate work. The results, however, can be very beautiful and can tell us much about life in the past.

If palaeontologists find a whole fossil skeleton in the rock they try not to disturb it. They coat it with sacking soaked in plaster and take it back to the laboratory to study. What kind of animal do you think owned this skeleton? (See page 48)

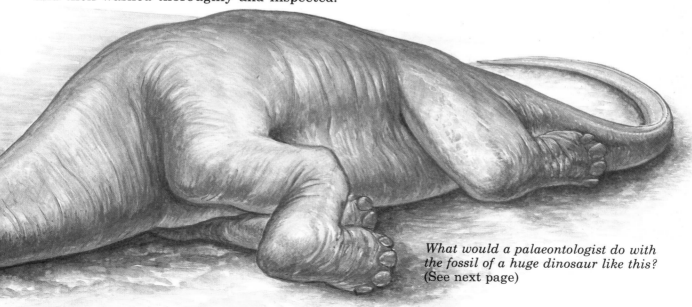

What would a palaeontologist do with the fossil of a huge dinosaur like this? (See next page)

How do we examine dinosaur bones?

The most impressive fossils are those of dinosaur bones. Unfortunately they are also amongst the rarest of fossils. They are usually found as single, isolated bones and it is very difficult to tell what kind of animal they came from. Sometimes, however, palaeontologists find whole dinosaur skeletons embedded in sedimentary rocks. These must be handled very delicately, removed bone-by-bone and brought to the laboratory for serious study.

What is a reconstruction?

Sometimes, if the skeleton is well exposed in the rock, the palaeontologists will leave it embedded, as on page 15. However, if the skeleton is a large one and has to be brought into the laboratory bone-by-bone, the palaeontologists and technicians may mount it. This means that the skeleton will stand in the same position as it would have been in the living animal, as on page 22. This is called a reconstruction. In a big reconstruction the skeleton has to be supported by a scaffolding of steel rods and girders.

What is a restoration?

For a reconstruction that is going on public display, the skeleton must look very smart. Sometimes missing bones are 'borrowed' from other skeletons. Sometimes we do not know what a missing part looks like so fake bones are put in. These substitutes are always based on what the palaeontologist thinks the missing bones would look like. This is to give people as complete an idea as possible of how the animal appeared.

To give an even better picture, the palaeontologists and technicians produce a restoration. This is a painting, or a model, or anything else that shows what the animal was like when it was alive.

To do this, the palaeontologist looks at the reconstructed skeleton and calculates from that where the soft parts would have been. Marks on the bones show how the muscles were attached. The shape of the rib-cage and the hips show the size of its lungs and intestines. Finally the palaeontologist visualizes the kind of skin texture that the animal must have had, and has an educated guess about the colour (the larger the animal the more likely it is to be a subdued colour). The resulting picture is the restoration.

Dinosaur bones are often found in a jumbled heap

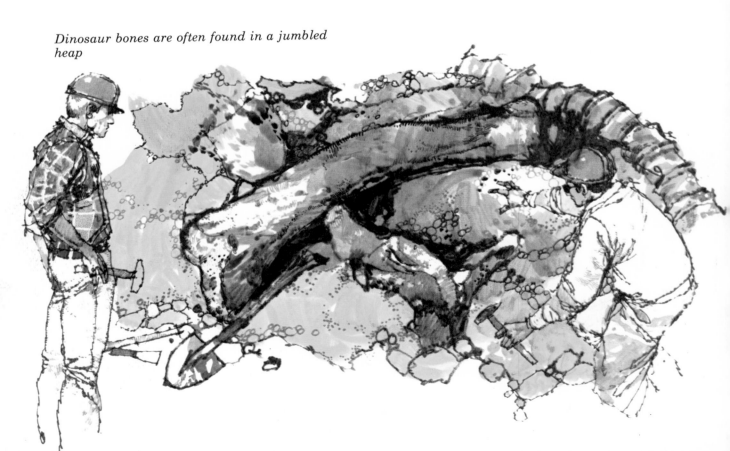

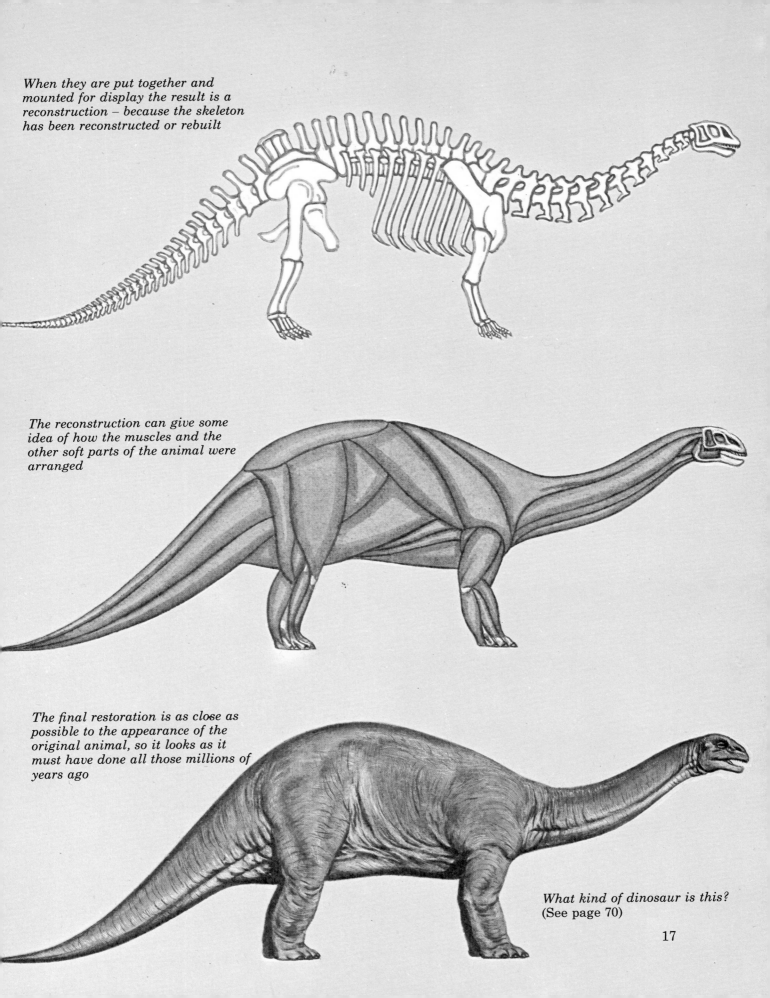

When they are put together and mounted for display the result is a reconstruction – because the skeleton has been reconstructed or rebuilt

The reconstruction can give some idea of how the muscles and the other soft parts of the animal were arranged

The final restoration is as close as possible to the appearance of the original animal, so it looks as it must have done all those millions of years ago

What kind of dinosaur is this? (See page 70)

17

How accurate are restorations?

If palaeontologists find a perfect skeleton, with every bone in place, the restoration that they can produce will be fairly accurate. However, even the best skeletons may have bits missing – and usually the most important bits. The most fragile part of a dinosaur skeleton is the skull, because it is very lightly built and made of very thin and delicate bones. Often the skull is crushed out of all recognition, or is completely lost. Then the palaeontologist can only guess at what the head of the animal looked like.

The skin is difficult to restore, too. Being soft it does not fossilize easily. However, sometimes where a dinosaur has rolled in the mud, it leaves a skin impression as a trace fossil (see page 13). In one or two instances the dead dinosaur had lain in the sun for a while before being buried and its skin had dried into a tough leather. This has fossilized and has shown us that a dinosaur's skin was a mass of small scales, and had a wrinkled leathery appearance.

Colour is always a matter of guesswork. The palaeontologist can look at the type of landscape that the animal lived in, and can work out what would be the best colour to camouflage it, but there will be no direct evidence.

What were early restorations like?

It was in the 1820s that dinosaur fossils were first recognized. One of the first dinosaurs to be described was *Iguanodon* in 1825.

Unfortunately the palaeontologists of the time had nothing to go on except a few bones, a handful of teeth and a strange-looking spike. The palaeontologists recognized the remains as coming from a giant reptile and they restored it as a kind of giant lizard.

In 1854 full-sized statues of *Iguanodon* and some of the other newly-discovered dinosaurs were built in the grounds of the Crystal Palace in south London (below). Since then palaeontologists have found complete skeletons of *Iguanodon*. We now know that the animal stood more like a kangaroo and that the odd-looking spike which was restored as a nose-horn in 1854 was actually the animal's thumb (inset).

Despite their inaccuracies the Crystal Palace statues are magnificent pieces of work and stand in the park to this day.

Who was the palaeontologist who first discovered Iguanodon and restored it like these statues? (See page 153)

Toothed Ichthyornis

Modern restoration of Ichthyornis

Can we tell how dinosaurs lived?

Hypsilophodon (below) was quite a small dinosaur. It was less than 2 metres (6 feet) long and lived in the early part of the Cretaceous period.

For almost 90 years palaeontologists restored it as a tree-living animal. The small first toe of the hind foot seemed to point backwards. This made the foot the same shape as the foot of a perching bird and would have enabled it to grasp thin branches. As well as that, the animal had the same build as the modern tree-kangaroo of Australia, so it looked quite well in a tree.

Then, in 1974, another palaeontologist looked at the remains and saw that the original reconstruction was wrong. The first toe did not point backwards and the whole leg seemed to be built for running, not climbing. Modern restorations show it as a running animal.

Climbing Hypsilophodon

How can restorations go wrong?

This bird (above) is called *Ichthyornis*. It was a sea bird and lived during the Cretaceous period, at the height of the age of dinosaurs. The top picture is how it has nearly always been restored. See the teeth in the beak? This is very unusual in a bird but it does sometimes happen. The palaeontologists found the jaw bone, complete with teeth, amongst the other bones of the bird. Another bird, the flightless *Hesperornis*, lived in the same seas at the same time and it definitely had teeth. So the palaeontologists happily restored *Ichthyornis* as a toothed sea bird, wondering if all sea birds of the Cretaceous period had teeth.

Recently, however, other palaeontologists have found that the toothed jaw-bone actually belonged to a swimming lizard of the time and not to the bird at all. More up-to-date restorations of *Ichthyornis* have no teeth.

Modern restoration of running Hypsilophodon

19

What can we tell from fossils?

We can discover a great deal about how ancient animals lived by looking at their fossils.

Palaeontologists do not usually find a single fossil sitting on its own in a sedimentary rock. There are usually many fossils present and this collection of fossils is called an assemblage. A palaeontologist can look at a fossil assemblage and work out the kind of landscape there was at the time a particular rock was laid down.

For example, the remains of a kind of giant newt are found in a bed of shale. The shale means that there was plenty of mud around at the time the newt lived. Also in the shale are carbonized remains of plants (see page 13). One plant is a horsetail with star-shaped leaves, another is a tree with a diamond-shaped pattern on the bark. Above and below the shale are beds of coal.

From this evidence we can work out that our giant newt lived in a muddy swamp, with forests all about, containing horsetails and trees with diamond-patterned bark. These conditions were common in the Carboniferous period.

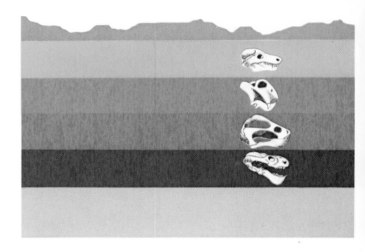

How else can we use fossils?

Undisturbed sedimentary rocks are youngest at the top and become older the deeper they go, so the fossils in the lowest sedimentary rocks are of animals that lived before the animals who left their remains in shallower rocks. By looking at how the fossils differ from one level of rocks to another, the palaeontologists can work out how life has changed on Earth as time has gone on.

There is another practical use to this. Once the palaeontologists have recognized which animals lived at which period, they can tell the age of any other rock in which they find similar remains. This is called 'correlation'.

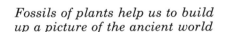

Fossils of plants help us to build up a picture of the ancient world

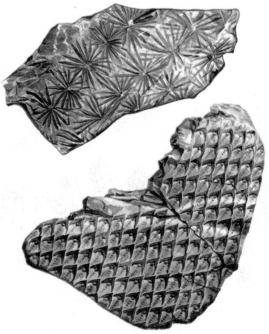

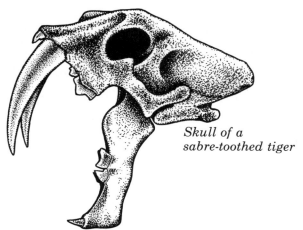

*Skull of a
sabre-toothed tiger*

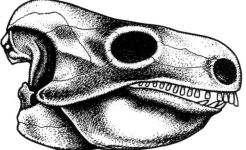

Skull of Diadectes, *an early reptile*

Can we tell how ancient animals lived?

A palaeontologist can look at a set of fossil-ized teeth and tell straight away what that animal ate. The sabre-toothed tiger (top) had long killing teeth and sharp meat-cutting teeth. It ate flesh. *Diadectes* (above), an early reptile, had weak peg-like teeth. It ate plants. *Iguanodon* (page 18) was first recognized as a plant-eating reptile because its teeth were identical to those of the plant-eating iguana lizard of today.

Animals that have the same sort of lifestyle and live in a similar environment tend to look the same – they have all developed the most efficient shape for a particular way of life. Look at these three swimming creatures (right). They are all very large, have the same shaped bodies, the same swimming limbs and the same kind of teeth. However, one is a fish, one a reptile and the other a mammal. We can compare the fossilized remains of ancient animals with more familiar animals and learn something about their lifestyles.

All these animals have similar shapes to enable them to live a fish-eating existence in the open ocean. This is called 'convergent evolution'

Dinichthys, *fish-eating fish.
Length 10 m (33 ft), Devonian period*

Tylosaurus,
*fish-eating reptile.
Length 7 m (23 ft),
Cretaceous period*

Basilosaurus,
*fish-eating whale.
Length 20 m (66 ft),
Eocene period*

21

Where can we see fossil collections?

What kind of dinosaur was this? (See page 83)

The best collections of fossils and mounted skeletons are found in museums.

Mounted skeletons (a) are always very impressive but museums also have other exhibits (b) showing life in the past, how it has changed through time and how we know about it. The staff there will always be very helpful if you ask them about things that puzzle you.

You are not always able to see all the work that goes on in a big natural history museum. Behind the scenes research is going on all the time (c). New fossils are always being discovered and palaeontologists are always working away, identifying them and cataloguing them.

In other departments there may be artists and model-makers (d), preparing exhibits and displays for the museum. These people have a very important job, taking the information that the palaeontologists have produced and turning it into a form that we can all understand.

All the fossils brought in will have to be catalogued and stored (e). They will have to be arranged so that the palaeontologists know

f

g

Can you make your own museum?

It is very simple to build a small museum of your own. All you need is some storage space and a file index.

If you find a fossil, you should always give it a number and write on a card what it is and where you found it. If you don't know what it is take it to your local museum. It may be something completely new!

The best way to store your collection is in small boxes, each one numbered so that you can find its entry in your index. They should be kept in a drawer to keep the dust off them. Anything really spectacular should be put in some sort of display cabinet so that you can show it off!

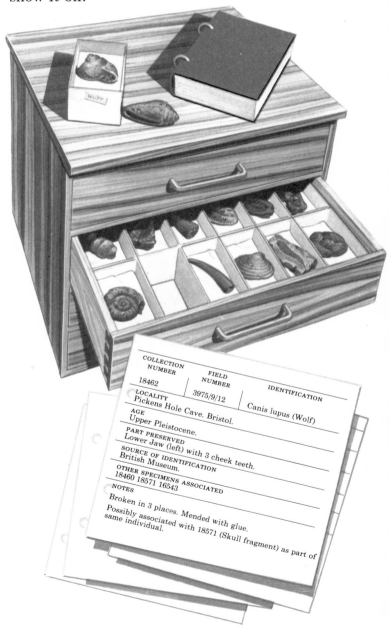

where to find them if they want to work on them or if they want to compare them with other fossils.

The technicians prepare and clean the new fossils, remove the surrounding rock and make them fit for study and display (f).

Make the most of the museums. Enjoy any trips from school or visit them while on holiday. Often, if you go with an organized group you will have the chance to handle interesting fossils and to look at them closely (g). Many famous palaeontologists have started in this way – looking at the wonderful collections of fossils that were on display in their local museums.

It is always a good idea to visit a local museum before you begin collecting fossils as the displays will probably show you the kinds of fossils that you can expect to find in that area and may show the types of rock in which they occur.

Don't be afraid to ask for advice. If you find an interesting fossil, take it along to your nearest museum. You will find someone there who will be delighted to help you find out what it is. There may even be a bookshop in your museum, and this will certainly sell books on fossils that will help you to identify your finds.

When did life appear?

We first see traces of life in rocks dating back to the Precambrian. We know that there were living things on the Earth 3 billion years ago — that is at about 21 minutes past the hour on our clock on page 10. At this time, the only living things would have been very simple seaweed-like plants.

Where did life come from?

That is a question we really cannot answer. Some scientists think that the chemicals that make up living things were formed in space and drifted down to Earth. Others say that they formed on Earth to start with.

The painting below shows what the Earth was like in its early days. Not a very pleasant place! We would not have been able to breathe the air because it contained gases, like ammonia and methane, and very little, if any, oxygen. The Earth's crust was still cooling and so volcanoes were erupting all the time. Steam from the volcanoes produced a perpetual rain. Thunder rumbled and the lightning flashed continuously through the downpour.

Scientists have been able to study these conditions in the laboratory. They boiled water, to represent the steam from volcanoes, and passed it through a mixture of ammonia and methane gas, to represent the ancient atmosphere. Then they passed electricity through it to represent the lightning. They found that this experiment produced the kind of chemicals that make up living things. However, they have not actually been able to produce life.

What were the first life-forms like?

The first living thing would have been a chemical molecule that could reproduce itself. It would have had the power to take in the raw chemicals dissolved in the water round about and put them together to build a complete replica of itself. This replica would also have had this power, and soon the early seas would have been full of these molecules. From then on, evolution would have built up these simple chemicals into more complex living things.

What is evolution?

Evolution is the process whereby animals and plants gradually change from one generation to another so that they can survive in changing conditions.

Usually a creature is very much like its parents. Sometimes, however, an animal or a plant grows up to be slightly different from its parents. If this difference makes it less able to survive, it will die out. However, if the difference makes it better able to survive, it will survive, and this difference will be passed on to its children. In this way living creatures can change from generation to generation. They will evolve.

What are early fossils like?

The first animals had no hard shells. They were just soft wriggly things so they could not leave any fossils. In some areas a kind of seaweed caught up mud particles in its fronds and the resulting mud heaps are sometimes found preserved in very ancient rocks.

The earliest good fossils lie in rocks of the very late Precambrian, about 680 million years ago, or about nine minutes to the hour on our time clock on page 10. These are the remains of soft creatures, like jellyfish and worms, and animals that seem to be the ancestors of the corals and segmented creatures to come. Most of these fossils are found in an area of Australia.

A selection of late Precambrian fossils. We do not often find fossils of such soft-bodied creatures

Medusina, *a jellyfish*

Dickinsonia, *a worm*

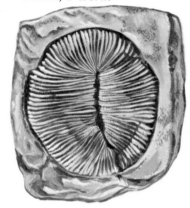

Spriggina, *a worm*

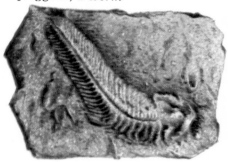

Charnia, *a sea pen*

How old are the first clear fossils?

Animals suddenly developed hard shells at the beginning of the Cambrian period, about 570 million years ago. Sedimentary rocks that were formed in the Cambrian, and in the following Ordovician and Silurian periods, are full of the fossils of all sorts of creatures.

All of these creatures lived in the sea. There was still no life on land. The sea bottom during Cambrian, Ordovician and Silurian times – or the Lower Palaeozoic era as geologists sometimes call this time – would have looked like the illustration below. There would have been many creatures that we do not know about. Not all the animals that ever lived left fossils behind. Many types of animals at this time would have had soft bodies, with no hard parts at all, such as the jellyfish and the worm in the picture.

What kinds of rocks contain these fossils?

The deep sea bottom was covered with very fine mud and so this eventually produced beds of shale. Shallower seas, close to the continents, had beds of sand and eventually formed sandstone. Sometimes there were so many animals living in one place that their dead shells covered the sea floor in a thick layer. These deposits would later form limestone.

What is a nautiloid?

A nautiloid is a creature like an octopus that lived inside a shell. Nautiloids are common in Lower Palaeozoic rocks. The earliest had long tapering cone-shaped shells, some of which were 3 metres (10 feet) in length. Later nautiloids of the Lower Palaeozoic had shells that were curved like cows' horns. Later still, in the Upper Palaeozoic, the shells became tightly coiled.

It is not until the Mesozoic era, the time of the dinosaurs, that the nautiloids become really important. By this time they had evolved into the ammonites and they abounded in the seas of the Triassic, Jurassic and Cretaceous periods. Every species was different, in the tightness of coiling or in the ornamentation. Geologists use them to work out the ages of Mesozoic rocks.

Two ammonites, Mesozoic nautiloids

Cardioceras

Hamites

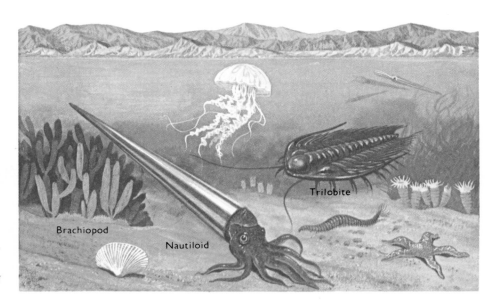

Brachiopod

Nautiloid

Trilobite

Lower Palaeozoic sea bottom with typical animal life

26

Trilobite fossils

Olenellus

Paradoxides

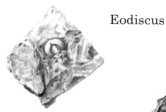

Eodiscus

Phacops

Calymene

What is a trilobite?

Amongst the most typical sea animals of the Lower Palaeozoic were the trilobites. These had jointed bodies and many jointed legs. They looked rather like woodlice. They had a large head shield – often with large eyes – a segmented body and usually a tail shield.

The early forms, such as *Olenellus* and *Paradoxides*, had no tail shield. The legs and antennae were very delicate and we hardly ever find these fossilized. The most common trilobite fossils are broken shell parts. When it was alive the animal grew by shedding its shell and growing another. The specimen of *Eodiscus*, above, is only the head shield.

Many trilobites could defend themselves by rolling up like armadillos and tucking in their vulnerable legs and antennae. The *Phacops* specimen is rolled up like this. They were mostly small but some were 50 centimetres (20 inches) long.

After the Lower Palaeozoic the trilobites began to fade away. At the end of the Palaeozoic they died out completely. There are no trilobites left today, instead, we have crabs, shrimps and lobsters.

Were there shellfish in the Lower Palaeozoic seas?

The shellfish of these early seas looked a bit like those of today but really they were totally different. They were the brachiopods and were in no way related to today's shellfish which are called bivalves. The reason that they look much the same is that they had identical lifestyles. This is called convergent evolution (see page 21).

The brachiopods had two shells, like the bivalves, but unlike the bivalves the shells were a top shell and a bottom shell – bivalves have a left shell and a right shell. The shells protected the animal inside from being washed around on the sea bottom and from being eaten by animals such as the nautiloids.

By the end of the Palaeozoic the brachiopods were becoming scarce as the bivalves developed. We still have them today, but there are very few left.

Brachiopod fossils

Conchidium

Orthis

Leptaena

Dielasma

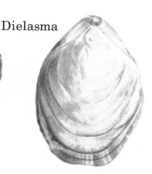

Were there corals then?

Corals appeared in Lower Palaeozoic times. These, however, were not the branching, reef-forming organisms that we know today. They were what the palaeontologists call 'solitary corals'. The best way of imagining them would be as a sea anemone growing in a horn-shaped shell. You have probably seen sea anemones in rock pools at the seaside – blobs of jelly with bunches of tentacles, attached to rocks. The sea anemones are very closely related to the corals and feed the same way by grabbing drifting food with their tentacles and pulling it into their stomachs.

As the Palaeozoic era progressed, more and more complicated types of coral appeared. The single horn-shaped shell branched into several shells, with a number of animals attached to the same mass. Eventually these evolved into forms that had each branch crammed against its neighbour to form a solid mass.

From this it was a short step to the types of coral that we get today in which all the individuals are growing on one another, the living ones building up new shells on the skeletons of their dead parents. This is how coral reefs form, and in tropical oceans there are entire islands made up of nothing but coral skeletons.

There were reefs in ancient times as well. However, these reefs were not only produced from corals. Many of the brachiopods (see page 27) grew attached to one spot on the sea floor. As they died their young grew on the skeletons of the older ones. The result was a reef made up of brachiopod shells growing upon one another. Many other different creatures lived and hid amongst the dead skeletons of these ancient reefs.

A solitary coral, Caninia, *of the Palaeozoic era*

Syringopora, *this Palaeozoic coral lived in large colonies forming coral reefs*

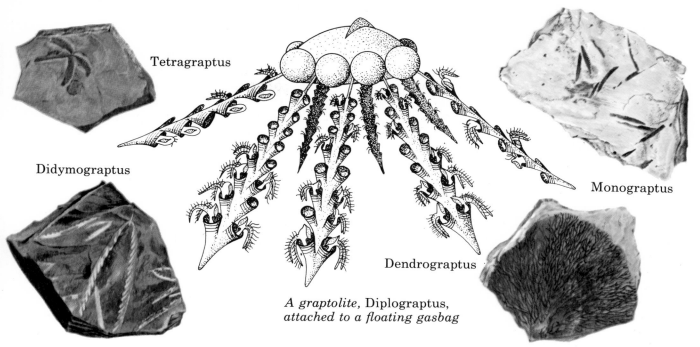

Tetragraptus

Didymograptus

Monograptus

Dendrograptus

A graptolite, Diplograptus, *attached to a floating gasbag*

What floated in the Lower Palaeozoic sea?

Graptolites were common, particularly in Ordovician and Silurian times. They were colonial organisms – that is, a number of individuals grew from a single stalk, or stipe. The animals lived in little hard cups that branched off the stipe. They floated in the ocean waters, either supported by a gasbag or attached to floating debris. When they died they sank to the bottom of the ocean.

This is why we often find them in shales that were formed from mud in the deepest basins of the world's oceans. Nothing could live in these deep basins so the graptolites that fell from above are usually the only fossils we find in these shales.

The earliest graptolites were many-branched and fan-shaped, such as *Dendrograptus*. As time went on they had fewer and fewer stipes. *Tetragraptus* had four stipes, while *Didymograptus* had two and *Monograptus* only one.

We find the different types in rocks that date from particular periods. In fact, the graptolites changed so quickly that we can be very accurate about the age of a bed in which we find a particular graptolite. They are the correlation fossils (see page 20) of the Ordovician and Silurian periods.

While all this was happening in the sea, what lived on land?

. . . *nothing*

What is a vertebrate?

Any animal with a backbone, and a skeleton inside its body, is a vertebrate. Nearly all the big animals that exist are vertebrates. They are the fish, the amphibians, the reptiles, the birds and the mammals. You and I are vertebrates, so it is not surprising that we think of the vertebrates as the most advanced and highly evolved creatures that ever lived.

From the fossils that we find in Palaeozoic rocks we can see that the vertebrates appeared fairly late in the Earth's history. The first were very primitive fish and their fossils are found in Silurian rocks. These eventually evolved into amphibians, then reptiles and finally mammals and birds.

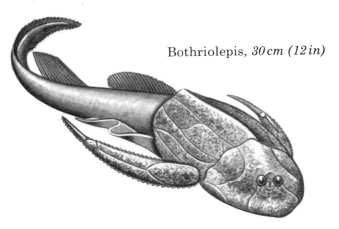

Bothriolepis, *30 cm (12 in)*

How long were the biggest of these armoured forms? (See page 21)

Amphioxus, *5 cm (2 in)*

What were the first fish like?

The earliest fish, like *Hemicyclaspis*, were not very different from *Amphioxus*. They had the same streamlined shape, with gills at one end and a tail for swimming at the other. These early fish had no jaws, but fed through a mouth that was like a sucker. The lamprey of today has the same kind of mouth.

The first fish with jaws lived in the Devonian period. *Bothriolepis* was an example. They were covered with armour at the front and some were quite fierce.

How did vertebrates evolve?

The creature shown here is *Amphioxus*. It is a kind of swimming worm that can still be seen today. It has gills at the front and a swimming tail at the rear, but the most important thing about it is a long, stiff bar of gristle that runs the length of the body and supports it. Creatures like this existed in the Lower Palaeozoic and the vertebrates evolved from them. The stiff bar eventually became the backbone and the rest of the skeleton developed from that.

Cladoselache, *1 m (3 ft)*

What were early skeletons made of?

The first skeletons, which consisted merely of a skull, a backbone, some ribs and, later, jaws, were not made from bone. They were made from cartilage – a springy, gristly material. Some of today's fish still have skeletons that are made from cartilage. These are the sharks and skates. In Devonian times there were primitive sharks that looked very much like those that we have today. *Cladoselache* was typical of these early sharks.

Hemicyclaspis, *20 cm (8 in)*

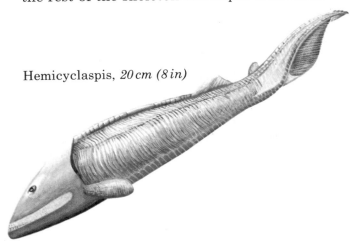

When did bone evolve?

The first creatures with bony skeletons appeared in the Devonian period – these were fish. There were two kinds of bony fish – the ray-finned fish and the lobe-finned fish.

The ray-finned fish had fan-shaped fins supported on fine bones that spread out from stumps on the body. They looked very much like modern fish and, indeed, evolved into the modern fish during Mesozoic times.

The fins of the lobe-finned fish were muscular lumps of flesh and bone, fringed by narrow bands of fin material. These fins were arranged in pairs along the lower part of the body. They led to the next step in the evolution of the vertebrates.

What were the first land-living vertebrates?

In Devonian times, the bony fish lived in shallow coastal waters, estuaries and rivers. The land was nearly all desert at this time. Occasionally the rivers dried out, and any fish living in them were left stranded. However, certain fish could still survive.

Eusthenopteron, *a lobe-finned fish, 30 cm (12 in)*

In those days the bony fish had lungs. This meant that, when all the oxygen in the water was used up, the fish could come to the surface and gulp down some more. Nowadays very few fish have lungs. The ancient lung has now evolved into a swim bladder – a bag of air inside the fish that helps it to float.

A lobe-finned fish, left out of the water, would have been able to pull itself across the dry land. It would have been able to spread its lobe fins to keep its body upright and it could have used them to heave itself across the mud to find some more water.

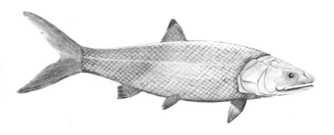

Caturus, *an early ray-finned fish, 60 cm (24 in)*

The ability to live on land evolved to enable the fish to continue as a water-living creature!

From this condition it would have been a short step, in evolutionary terms, to a land-living animal.

What was happening on the land?

Plants had already started growing on land in the Devonian. They were very simple moss-like plants but they would have covered much of the river-bank areas close to the water. These plants would have added oxygen to the atmosphere, allowing animal life to leave the water and live on land.

Primitive Devonian plants

Drepanophycus   Psilophyton

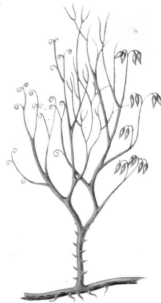

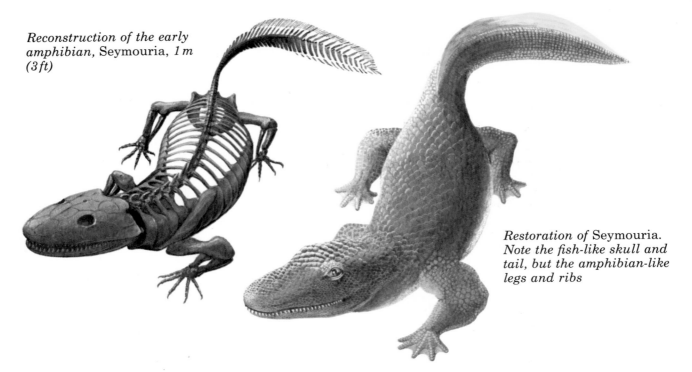

Reconstruction of the early amphibian, Seymouria, *1 m (3 ft)*

Restoration of Seymouria. *Note the fish-like skull and tail, but the amphibian-like legs and ribs*

What is an amphibian?

Once the fish had left the water and were able to live on land for a time, the amphibians soon developed from them. Amphibians are creatures that can live on land but must spend their early stages in the water. Frogs, toads, newts and salamanders are modern amphibians which spend their water-living early stages as tadpoles.

The first amphibians appeared late in the Devonian period. Their skeletons were very similar to skeletons of fish – with a skull and a tail like a fish. However, they had legs which had evolved from the fleshy and bony lobes of the lobe-finned fish. They also had a strong rib-cage to support the lungs and enable them to work out of the water.

As the Devonian period ended and the Carboniferous period began, the amphibians evolved into all sorts of forms. The age of fish gave way to the age of amphibians.

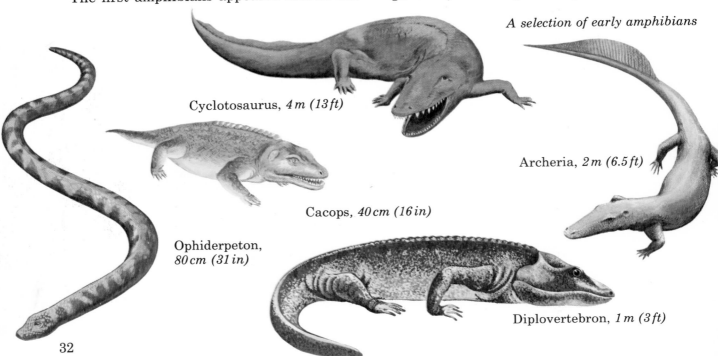

A selection of early amphibians

Cyclotosaurus, *4 m (13 ft)*

Archeria, *2 m (6.5 ft)*

Cacops, *40 cm (16 in)*

Ophiderpeton, *80 cm (31 in)*

Diplovertebron, *1 m (3 ft)*

Where did the early amphibians live?

The landscape of the Carboniferous period was quite different from that of the Devonian period. The Devonian was a time of deserts, with plants growing only in the damp places around lakes and streams. The Carboniferous was a time of lush forests and humid swamps that thrived in the moist, mild, humid climate.

By this time plants had evolved into huge trees. These trees were not like the trees we have today, but were very primitive. They were more like ferns and horsetails than anything else we know. Some of them grew to heights of 30 metres (98 feet) or more. These plants formed forests on the deltas and swamps that lay around the edges of most of the continents. Beneath the shade of these trees, there was a thick undergrowth of ferns and deep reed-beds of giant horsetails grew in the water. Scorpions, millipedes, spiders and giant insects flourished in these conditions, and so did the amphibians.

We can see how the early amphibians lived by looking at their shapes. Many, like *Diplovertebron*, lived by scrambling over the rotting vegetation and snapping up the giant dragonflies and cockroaches that lived there. Some, like *Archeria*, were long and thin and swam in the shallow waters feeding on fish. Some of these water-living types, such as *Ophiderpeton*, had lost their legs altogether and lived like eels. Others were huge monsters, cruising the swamp waters like alligators, preying on the smaller amphibians. Such a creature was *Cyclotosaurus*.

As the Carboniferous period passed into the next period, the Permian, the forests died away and the deserts spread out once more. Most of the amphibians retreated to an almost complete water-living existence but some became much better at living on dry land. Some of the dry land animals, such as *Cacops*, had armour plates. They were not very successful and soon died out. Turn to the next page to discover what replaced them.

The lush swamps of the Carboniferous, home to the early amphibians. When all this vegetation died it eventually became coal

Hylonomus, *20 cm (8 in).*
The earliest known reptile

Where did the reptiles come from

The reptiles evolved from the amphibians living in the swamps and forests of the Carboniferous period. The first reptiles looked just like the amphibians of the time and probably spent much of their time in the water.

The big difference between them and the amphibians was in the eggs that they laid. Reptile eggs were laid on the land and not in the water. They were covered by a tough shell so that they did not dry out, and the baby reptile was able to develop inside the egg until it was ready to break out. It hatched fully able to take care of itself in the outside world without going through a tadpole stage first.

The early reptiles had stronger legs than the amphibians of the time. The shoulder bones and hip bones were fixed more sturdily into the skeleton. The toes were longer and this gave them a better grip on the ground.

All these features made them better able to live on land than the amphibians. When the forests of the Carboniferous period died away they were able to live quite easily in the deserts of the Permian. At first the reptiles had to compete with the land-living amphibians but the amphibians soon became fewer and fewer and left the reptiles as the masters.

What kinds of reptiles were there?

Once the reptiles became successful they evolved into all sorts of different kinds. Some ate plants while others ate meat.

The plant-eaters, like *Scaphonyx* (below), usually had quite large bodies compared with the meat-eaters. This is because an animal needs a lot more intestine to digest tough plant material than to digest meat. A meat-eating animal is usually quite small and light so that it can run after the plant-eating animals to kill them.

Most of the varied reptile types of the Permian became extinct and there is nothing like them left today. However, *Scaphonyx* has a modern relative in the lizard-like tuatara of New Zealand.

In Permian times, the two most important types of reptile were the thecodonts and the mammal-like reptiles. These evolved into totally different groups of animals.

Scaphonyx, *2 m (6.5 ft).*
An early plant-eating reptile

34

What was a thecodont?

The thecodonts looked a bit like crocodiles. The name 'thecodont' means 'socket-toothed' and this refers to the fact that each tooth was embedded in a socket in the jaw.

Many of the thecodonts lived in water and they grew long hind legs and strong tails to help them swim. They eventually evolved into the crocodiles. However, others came out on to land where their strong hind legs and tails allowed them to walk on their hind feet. These would eventually evolve into dinosaurs in the Triassic period.

Dimetrodon, *2 m (6.5 ft).*
A meat-eating pelycosaur

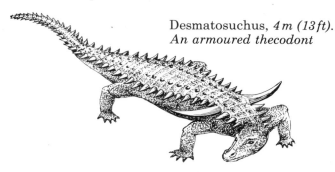

Desmatosuchus, *4 m (13 ft).*
An armoured thecodont

What was a mammal-like reptile?

The most successful reptiles of the Permian period were the mammal-like reptiles. The most primitive of these were the pelycosaurs. They looked like big lizards with huge sail-like fins on their backs. There were both plant-eating and meat-eating pelycosaurs.

The sail was used to keep the animal warm or cool. In the early morning it could stand with its sail facing the sun and warm up quickly. When it was too warm it could turn its sail into the wind to cool off. Mammals, nowadays, can keep warm or cool by warming or cooling the blood inside their bodies. The pelycosaurs' fin arrangement was probably an early stage in this.

The more advanced mammal-like reptiles began to look very much like mammals. There were both plant-eating and meat-eating types of these as well. The plant-eating forms were often as big as cows while the meat-eaters were smaller and swifter.

In meat-eating mammal-like reptiles the teeth were of different sizes. There were killing teeth at the front and meat-shearing teeth at the back – just like a dog's. They also had furry coats and could alter their body heat by the amount of food they ate.

They evolved into mammals in the Triassic period. The first mammals were tiny, and the only large animals left on land in the Triassic were the thecodont reptiles.

Cynognathus, *2 m (6.5 ft).*
A meat-eating mammal-like reptile

35

Triassic landscape showing the dry conditions and some of the early dinosaurs

How did Triassic dinosaurs live?

The Triassic period – when the dinosaurs first evolved – was a time of deserts. We know this because of the huge deposits of sand that collected at the time. These eventually turned to great beds of sandstone that have unmistakable traces of sand dunes in them. They also contain footprints showing where two-footed animals walked across the sand, and sometimes complete skeletons where an unlucky animal was buried by a sandstorm. Many different kinds of reptiles lived in these deserts – just like the lizards and snakes of the deserts today – and the earliest dinosaurs were meat-eaters that preyed on them.

Across the deserts, rivers and streams would have flowed, probably drying up in the dry season. Oases of ferns and coniferous trees would have lined these rivers. Early dinosaurs would have lived here.

What was the world like then?

If you saw the Triassic world from space you would not have recognized it. None of the continents were in the same place as they are today. In fact, they were all crammed together in one big supercontinent that we now call Pangaea. A huge ocean called Panthalassa covered the rest of the Earth and a deep offshoot from it, called the Tethys Sea, cut into the continent, almost dividing it in two.

Broad, shallow seas lapped the edges of this continent along the edge of the Tethys, but there were mountains along the other coasts of Pangaea. Other mountain chains had been formed in earlier times, when pieces of continent pushed together. At this time the mountains were being worn down by the wind and the rain, their rocks turning into the sand that spread across the lowland deserts.

Where do we find Triassic dinosaurs?

Most Triassic dinosaur fossils have been found in central and eastern United States, the British Isles, northern Europe and South Africa. Northern Europe, at this time, lay by the shores of a shallow sea. The desert nearby had many shallow lakes that dried out giving beds of salt. The uplands surrounding these lakes contained many limestone caves in which animals sheltered. Dinosaur remains are often found in these cave deposits.

In the desert sandstones of South Africa some of the early dinosaurs have been found curled up as though asleep. This shows that they slept away the hottest, driest months just as crocodiles do nowadays.

Map of the world during the Triassic period, 225–195 million years ago

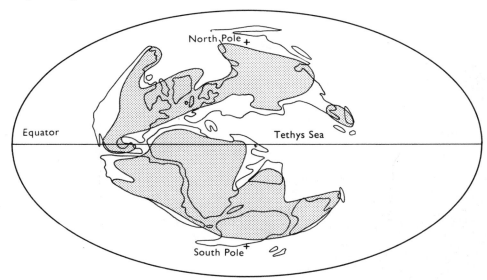

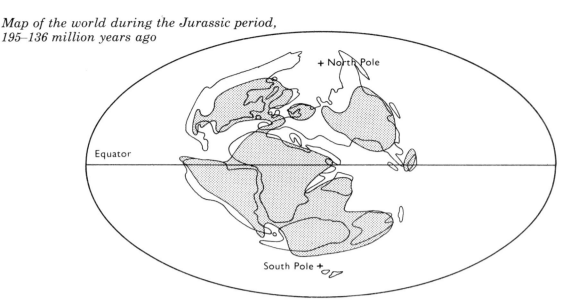

Map of the world during the Jurassic period, 195–136 million years ago

North Pole

Equator

South Pole

How did Jurassic dinosaurs live?

The Jurassic period saw the great expansion of the dinosaurs. They became the most important group of land animals at that time. Where there were deserts during the Triassic there were now lush forests and swamps. Tropical plants grew almost everywhere and there was enough to feed a large number of huge plant-eating animals. Meat-eaters flourished as well, since there were plenty of plant-eating animals for them to eat.

What was the world like then?

Pangaea had begun to break up. North America was breaking away from South America and from Europe, so the Atlantic Ocean was born. The splitting of the supercontinent opened up new seaways and vast areas of shallow sea spread across the lowlands. These brought moist climates deep into the new continents and so produced the forests that replaced the Triassic deserts. Huge reptiles lived in these shallow seas too, although these were not dinosaurs. Other reptiles flew in the skies above the warm seas and the forests.

Where do we find Jurassic dinosaurs?

As at other times, most Jurassic sedimentary rocks were formed in water so we most often find fossils of creatures that lived in the sea. The only time that we get a fossil of a land animal is when it fell into a river and its body was washed down to a lake or the sea. Because of this we know more about the land animals that lived by the water's edge than we do about land animals that lived inland or in the mountains.

The Mid-West of the United States has good dinosaur fossils. This area was a broad plain between the mountains and the sea during Jurassic times. Rivers flowed slowly over the plain and dinosaurs abounded in the forests along the river banks.

East Africa had the same sort of landscape and the Jurassic rocks there contain the same types of dinosaur fossils as the United States.

Germany was a shallow sea, with strings of wooded islands cutting off quiet lagoons. Small dinosaurs, flying reptiles and the first birds are fossilized in the lagoon deposits here.

A shallow inlet reached across southern England in the Upper Jurassic and the forests on its shores were roamed by dinosaurs. The rest of the British Isles was covered by shallow sea and the fossils of many sea reptiles lie in the Jurassic rocks of central England.

A curious deposit of Jurassic dinosaurs was found in 1976. These lay 4,200 metres (13,700 feet) above sea level in the Himalayas of Tibet. They were thrust up to that altitude when the continent of India collided with the rest of Asia after the dinosaurs became extinct.

Szechuan province in central China is particularly rich in Jurassic fossils, with entire beds of rock that seem to consist only of dinosaur remains.

All the sites in the world where Jurassic dinosaurs have been discovered have fossils of the same kinds of animals. This proves that the new continents were still joined together and the animals could move about easily.

Opposite *The creatures of the British seas*

Above *The misty swamps of Jurassic North America*

Below *The lagoons and islands of southern Germany*

Map of the world during the Cretaceous period,
136–65 million years ago

North Pole

Equator

South Pole +

How did Cretaceous dinosaurs live?

Things were changing in Cretaceous times. The climate was beginning to change and, at the same time, the plants altered. Up to now most plants had been ferns, cycads and conifers. Now, at the end of the Cretaceous the flowering plants evolved and thrived.

For the first time, different climates occurred in different parts of the world. There were coal forests in Alaska and Siberia while deserts lay in Mongolia and China.

Towards the end of the Cretaceous, the climate became seasonal. Instead of the same conditions prevailing all year round, there were distinct cold, dry, warm or wet seasons.

What was the world like then?

By the end of the Cretaceous the super-continent of Pangaea had broken up and the individual continents were spreading out over the Earth. There were very large areas of shallow seas at this time – even larger than those of the Jurassic. These seas were very rich in microscopic animals. When these died their skeletons sank to the bottom and collected in thick beds of limy mud. Today this mud has become the chalk that we can see in the white cliffs of Dover, as well as in northern Europe and Kansas in the United States.

Where do we find Cretaceous dinosaurs?

The most famous site for Lower Cretaceous dinosaur fossils is southern England. This is the area in which 19th century palae-ontologists first found dinosaur remains.

The arm of the sea that had covered this region in Jurassic times had, by now, become a huge lake. The plants that lined the shore were not much different from those that existed during the Jurassic. In the Upper Cretaceous the plants changed to ones that we would recognize today, and their fossils, along with fossils of the dinosaurs that lived amongst them, have been found in many places of the world.

The most famous Upper Cretaceous fossil sites are in the western part of North America. This was the scene of a great 'dinosaur rush' during the late 19th century, when palaeontologists set out on expeditions into unmapped areas of the North American interior. They had to fight hostile Indians, and sometimes each other, to try to bring back better dinosaur remains than anybody else. The other great Upper Cretaceous dinosaur sites are in Mongolia and China. These were not discovered until well into the 20th century.

The Cretaceous period saw the end of the dinosaurs. It also saw the end of the great swimming and flying reptiles, and a great many other creatures that lived in the sea. After that it was the time of the mammals.

Southern England in Lower Cretaceous times. What are the animals shown here? (See pages 85 and 120)

How did dinosaurs walk?

Crouch down on the floor and stick your knees out at the side. Put your hands down flat and stick out your elbows. Now try to walk like this. Not easy, is it? This is how amphibians, like newts, and small reptiles, like lizards, move about. It's all right for them. They can support their light bodies in this way.

Now, keeping your hands and your feet apart, straighten your arms and legs and walk again. A bit easier? Heavier reptiles, like crocodiles and the later thecodonts walked like this. This is what palaeontologists call the semi-upright stance.

Finally, bring your hands together, and your feet together, under your body and walk, keeping your arms and legs straight. You should find this easiest of all, as this is how mammals walk. It is also the way that the dinosaurs walked. They could support their heavy bodies quite easily like this, carrying their weight on top of a set of straight legs.

The mammal-like stance was perfected by the dinosaurs long before the big mammals came into being.

How do we know how an animal walked?

The shape of the hip bones tells us. An animal that holds its limbs out at the side carries its weight slung between them. The leg bone is plugged into a rigid cup in the hip bone to take the weight. An animal that walks with its legs held beneath it does not need this strength at that joint. The leg bone just fits into a gap in the hip bones with a small bony shelf above it to prevent it from popping out.

Something huge, like an enormous 80-tonne *Brachiosaurus*, could not have moved if it had lizard-like limbs. They could not have supported the great weight slung between them. The belly would have dragged on the ground. The body would also have had to be long and flexible so that it could twist from side to side, throwing the limbs forward and back. The skeletons make it clear that this did not happen.

The straight legs and complex hip arrangement allowed some of the heavy plant-eating dinosaurs, like *Corythosaurus*, to walk on their hind feet. They could not have done this with a sprawling gait.

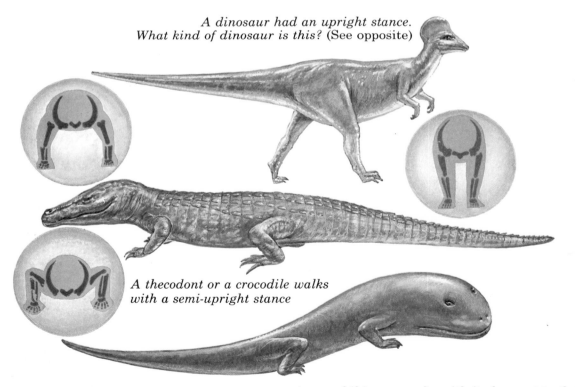

A dinosaur had an upright stance.
What kind of dinosaur is this? (See opposite)

A thecodont or a crocodile walks with a semi-upright stance

An amphibian sprawls, with its legs out to the side

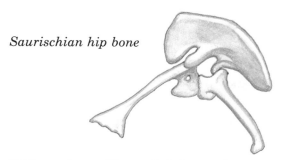

Saurischian hip bone

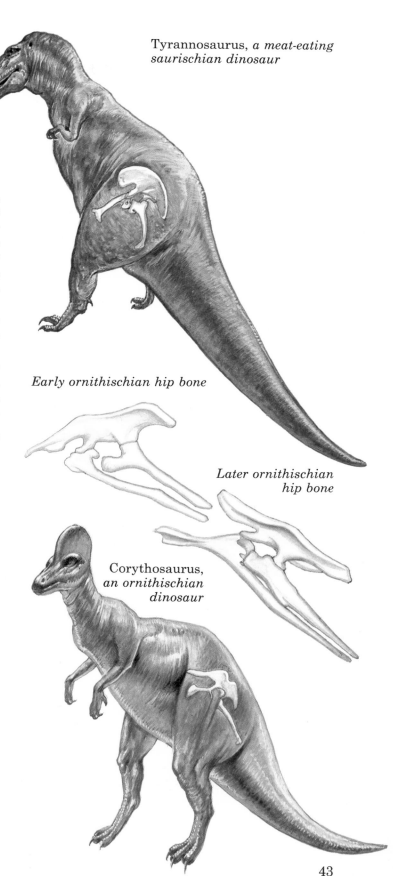

Tyrannosaurus, *a meat-eating saurischian dinosaur*

Early ornithischian hip bone

Later ornithischian hip bone

Corythosaurus, *an ornithischian dinosaur*

What is a lizard-hipped dinosaur?

We can divide the dinosaurs into two groups, depending on the positions of the bones of the hip. The first group is called the saurischia – the lizard-hipped dinosaurs. The hip is arranged like that of a lizard, with all the bony parts spreading away from the socket where the leg is attached. This is a very simple shape and the first dinosaurs all had this kind of hip.

All the meat-eating dinosaurs were lizard-hipped, from the tiny *Compsognathus* to mighty *Tyrannosaurus*.

The rest of the lizard-hipped dinosaurs were the long-necked plant-eating dinosaurs called the sauropods. A plant-eating animal needs a much larger intestine to digest its food than a meat-eating animal. The shape of the lizard-like hip meant that this great volume of intestine had to be carried well forward in the body. The first plant-eaters were too unbalanced to stand on their hind legs and took up a four-footed stance.

What is a bird-hipped dinosaur?

The second group of dinosaurs is called the ornithischia – the bird-hipped dinosaurs. These were all plant-eaters. In the simplest form of bird-hip, the pubis (the bone that sticks down and forward in the lizard-hipped dinosaur) pointed backwards. This made room for all the intestines that a plant-eater needed. The animal's weight could then be balanced nicely between its hind legs and it could walk on its two hind feet.

The later two-footed plant-eaters like *Iguanodon* and *Corythosaurus* had a more complicated bird-like hip. Here the pubis still pointed backwards but part of it extended forward to help support the animal's weight.

The armoured plant-eating dinosaurs were all descended from the two-footed forms and were all bird-hipped as well.

43

Did dinosaurs lay eggs?

We are quite sure that dinosaurs did lay eggs as we have found fossils of nests full of them. The first dinosaur eggs to be found were those of the horned dinosaur *Protoceratops*. A scientific expedition to Mongolia found these back in 1924. The dinosaur's nest consisted of a shallow pit scooped out of the ground, and several were found in the area.

Since then, eggs of the big, long-necked sauropod dinosaurs have been found. Palaeontologists have discovered eggs of *Hypselosaurus* in France. These eggs were 30 centimetres (12 inches) long, which is not very big for an animal with a length of 12 metres (39 feet). The eggs could not possibly have been any bigger, however, because the larger an egg is, the thicker must be its shell or it would collapse. A baby animal would not have been able to break through the shell of an egg that was any larger than this. Baby dinosaurs must have been very small and very weak when they hatched. Does this mean that the parents looked after them for a time?

The answer to this came with the discovery of dinosaur nests in Canada in 1979. They were nests of the duck-billed dinosaur *Maiasaura*. The nests were made of mud and were 1.5 metres (5 feet) high and 3 metres (10 feet) in diameter. They contained skeletons of partly grown youngsters. If the young stayed in the nest until they were this age they must have been looked after by the parent dinosaurs.

The dinosaurs may have had quite a complicated family life. They may have moved about in herds with the adult dinosaurs on the outside of the herd to protect the young in the middle.

Protoceratops *at the nest*

Were dinosaurs warm-blooded?

When we talk about a warm-blooded animal we mean an animal, like a mammal or a bird, that can control its body temperature. Mechanisms within its body keep the temperature the same all the time. To do this the body must take in a great deal of energy in the form of food.

A cold-blooded animal, on the other hand, stays at the same temperature as its surroundings. When the weather is cool, it becomes cool and sluggish. When the weather is warm, it becomes warm and active. This kind of life does not need nearly so much food. Reptiles and amphibians are cold-blooded.

Some palaeontologists claim that the dinosaurs were warm-blooded like mammals. Others argue violently that they were not. It is one of the main points of disagreement in palaeontology today.

Those who believe in warm-blooded dinosaurs say that the way they moved about on straight legs, and the way they looked after their young, suggests that they were warm-blooded. They also claim to have found microscopic structures in dinosaur bones that only form in warm-blooded animals.

Palaeontologists who think the dinosaurs were cold-blooded, think that a big dinosaur could not possibly have eaten enough food in the day for a warm-blooded lifestyle.

They may both be right. The big plant-eaters may have been cold-blooded, while the smaller meat-eaters may have been warm-blooded. We don't really know.

Brachiosaurus *shown as a cold-blooded animal, slow and lumbering*

Brachiosaurus *shown as a warm-blooded animal, swift and active*

Which do you think is correct? The palaeontologists don't know!

45

Protosuchus, *an early thecodont*

How did dinosaurs evolve?

At the end of the Permian the mammal-like reptiles were the main land-living animals. The other main group of reptiles, the thecodonts, lived mostly in the water. They looked rather like today's crocodiles. As they lived in the water they evolved long hind legs that helped them to swim and also a long swimming tail.

In the Triassic the mammal-like reptiles began to die out. Soon they were all extinct, leaving only their descendants, the mammals, behind. The thecodonts were then able to live on land. Their long hind legs and tail meant that it was easier for them to walk on their hind legs, using the tail stuck out behind as a balance.

From this point it was a very small step, in evolution, to the first of the meat-eating dinosaurs. Four different evolutionary lines sprang from the thecodonts: the lizard-hipped saurischians and the bird-hipped ornithischians (two groups of dinosaur), the pterosaurs or flying reptiles, and the crocodiles. The crocodiles stayed very much like their ancestors and have not altered very much to this day.

The lizard-hipped dinosaurs soon split into two groups. The first group were the meat-eaters and these kept the original two-footed design. They became the huge and heavy carnosaurs, and the smaller and swifter coelurosaurs. The second group were the plant-eating sauropods. These moved about on all fours and became some of the largest animals to walk the Earth. They took up the four-footed stance because the big body that they needed to digest plants had to be kept well forward of the lizard-like hips and they could not balance on their hind legs.

The bird-hipped dinosaurs were all plant-eaters. The earliest of these were two-footed. The bird-like hip allowed the large bodies to balance over their hind legs. Later bird-hipped dinosaurs became armoured and four-footed. The stegosaurs had a series of vertical plates on their backs and spikes on their tails. The plates may have been armour, but some palaeontologists suggest that they helped to warm the blood, like the sails of the pelycosaurs. The ankylosaurs evolved from the early stegosaurs and these had backs that were shielded by a heavy patchwork of bony plates. The last group of dinosaurs to evolve were the ceratopsians. These had all their armour on their faces. A bony shield covered the head and a horn, or several horns, stuck out of this. All these dinosaurs died out at the end of the Cretaceous period.

Euparkeria, *a later land-living thecodont*

RELATIONSHIPS OF DIFFERENT TYPES OF DINOSAURS

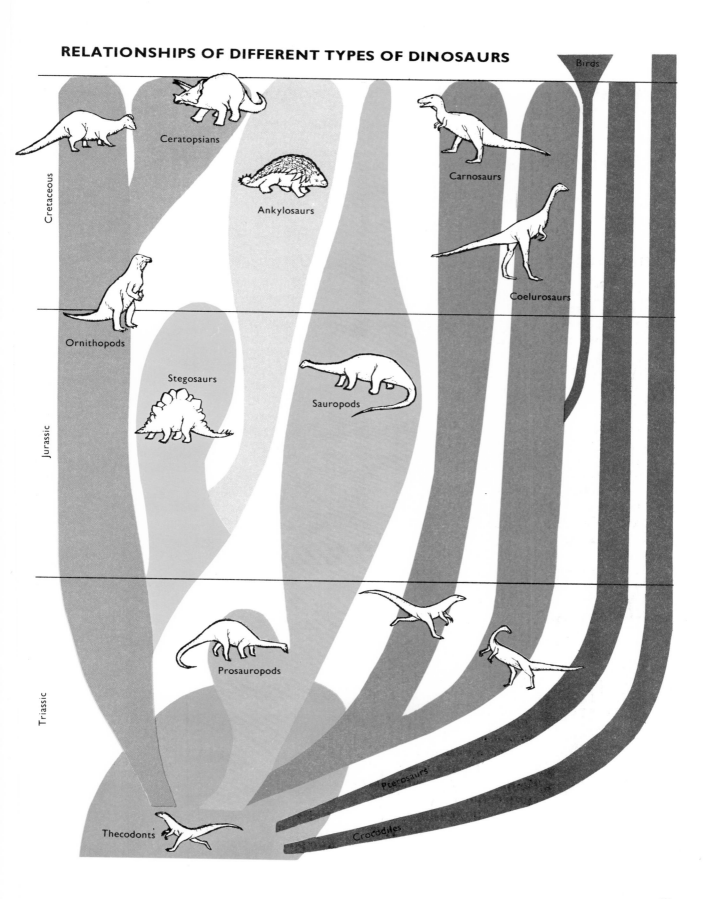

What is a coelurosaur?

The meat-eating dinosaurs were all lizard-hipped. Some were very large, but some were quite small. The large and small meat-eaters belonged to two distinct lines. The large ones were the carnosaurs and the smaller ones were the coelurosaurs.

The primitive coelurosaurs were very similar to their ancestors – the swift, meat-eating thecodonts – being lightly-built and fleet of foot. During the Triassic period a number of different coelurosaur groups evolved, but the main one was that to which *Coelophysis* belonged. It was this group that survived into the Jurassic period and produced the various types of coelurosaurs that lived through Jurassic and Cretaceous times.

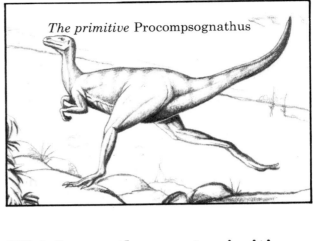

The primitive Procompsognathus

Which was the most primitive coelurosaur?

We cannot answer this question because we have not found fossils of every creature that ever lived. The most primitive coelurosaur that we know about is called *Procompsognathus*. It lived in Germany in Upper Triassic times. It still had five fingers on each hand – something unusual amongst meat-eating dinosaurs – but the feet already only had three toes.

FAMILY TREE OF THE COELUROSAURS

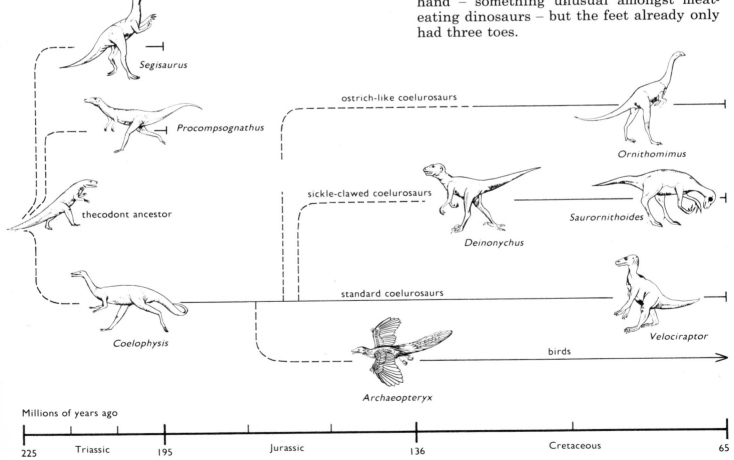

Segisaurus

Procompsognathus

thecodont ancestor

ostrich-like coelurosaurs

Ornithomimus

sickle-clawed coelurosaurs

Deinonychus

Saurornithoides

standard coelurosaurs

Velociraptor

Coelophysis

birds

Archaeopteryx

Millions of years ago

| 225 | Triassic | 195 | Jurassic | 136 | Cretaceous | 65 |

Which is the best-known?

Without a doubt the best-known coelurosaur is a 3-metre (10-feet) long Upper Triassic form from New Mexico called *Coelophysis*.

In 1881 dozens of skeletons of this creature were found all piled together in one place. It took the palaeontologists quite some time to sort them all out! It seems that they lived and travelled around in large herds. In other areas of Upper Triassic sandstones great numbers of their footprints have been found, again suggesting herds moving across the deserts.

The head of *Coelophysis* was quite long and the neck was very flexible. The tail was also very long but it would have been quite stiff to balance the animal as it ran. The forelimbs were about half the length of the hindlimbs and its fingers had been reduced to three – fewer than the more primitive *Procompsognathus*.

Coelophysis shows many features shared by the other coelurosaurs. It had quite large eye-sockets, suggesting that it had keen eyesight. This would be expected in an animal that spent all of its time hunting. Its bones were delicate and quite thin. This helped to keep down the weight of the animal so that it could run quite quickly. The bones of the lower leg were longer than the thigh. This is often found in running animals, where the leg muscles are concentrated in the upper leg and work the rest of the leg by tendons. This means that the lower leg is kept quite light and can be moved quickly. We can see this in running animals today, such as horses and ostriches.

Coelophysis *showing its meat-eating teeth*

Compsognathus, *60 mm (24 in) long*

Archaeopteryx, *a feathered coelurosaur or the first bird? The palaeontologists cannot agree*

Which was the smallest meat-eater?

The smallest coelurosaur that we know is *Compsognathus*. It was about the size of a chicken and lived in southern Germany in Upper Jurassic times. It had only two fingers on each hand. The first skeleton was found with lizard bones in the stomach.

What evolved from these coelurosaurs?

If you took the skeleton of *Compsognathus* and covered it in feathers you would end up with a very strange looking animal indeed – half dinosaur, half bird. Yet an animal just like this lived in southern Germany in Jurassic times. In fact, there have been five specimens of this curious creature discovered in the same rocks as *Compsognathus* in the last century.

It is called *Archaeopteryx* and it is regarded by some scientists as a feathered dinosaur and by others as the first bird. The feathers that were attached to the dinosaur-like skeleton formed a pair of wings that are very similar to those of a modern bird, except that they had three clawed fingers. They also fringed the long bony tail. The body was covered by smaller feathers. The head, however, was not bird-like at all, having toothed jaws instead of a beak. Whether or not *Archaeopteryx* was the first bird, there is no doubt that the birds did evolve from the coelurosaurs in the Jurassic period.

Skeleton of Archaeopteryx *fossilized in very fine-grained limestone. Note how clearly the feathers show*

Ornithomimus, *an ostrich dinosaur*

The toothless skull must have given it a very bird-like appearance. The big eyes show how alert it must have been

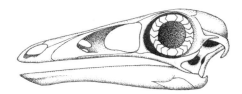

The three-fingered hand must have been very useful in finding food

Were all coelurosaurs small animals?

The coelurosaurs were small animals compared with the other meat-eating animals of the Jurassic and Cretaceous periods – the carnosaurs. However, some were quite large. One particular group of coelurosaurs were about the size of ostriches. In fact they must have looked rather like ostriches, with their long legs and necks and their squat bodies. Palaeontologists call these the ostrich dinosaurs.

A typical ostrich dinosaur was *Ornithomimus*. It had a length of about 3.5 metres (12 feet) and must have held its head about 2 metres (6.5 feet) above the ground. It had fairly long arms for a coelurosaur and each hand had three long fingers.

The ostrich dinosaurs arrived quite late on the dinosaur scene. They may have evolved in the Upper Jurassic as an ostrich-like form has been found in the Upper Jurassic of north Africa. However, they are better known from the Upper Cretaceous period, with different types found in North America, Europe and Asia. They were amongst the last of the dinosaurs.

How did the ostrich dinosaurs live?

The easy answer is that they lived like ostriches, emus and cassowaries. They must have done. Look at their legs, their necks, their tiny heads. We have already seen that animals that live in a similar way all tend to look very much alike. It was no different amongst the dinosaurs.

The narrow jaws had no teeth – like the beak of a bird. They probably ate many different things – seed-cones, small reptiles and insects, and possibly the eggs of other dinosaurs. Their long hands seem to have been suitable for grasping or even digging. They could not have fought off an enemy, but relied on their long legs and their speed for escape.

Some ostrich dinosaurs seem to have lived in herds in open country, like ostriches, while others lived in deep forests and jungles, like cassowaries.

The sickle-claw lowered for action

Deinonychus, *the sickle-clawed killer from Lower Cretaceous North America*

Which was the fiercest dinosaur?

We used to think that the big carnosaurs like *Tyrannosaurus* were the most ferocious creatures that ever lived. However, since the 1960s new discoveries have made us think again.

Palaeontologists discovered the skeleton of a big coelurosaur in Montana in 1964. And this creature must have been a living horror. It was between 3 and 4 metres (10 and 13 feet) long and stood a little over 1 metre (3 feet) high. It had quite a small body, balanced on strong running legs by a long stiff tail. Its head was quite large for the size of body and the jaws had sharp teeth. But its most alarming feature was its claw. It walked on two toes of its hind foot and the third had become a great slashing sickle-shaped talon. When walking, or running, this claw was lifted clear of the ground. When the animal was fighting it must have stood on one leg, balanced by its long waving tail, holding on to its prey with its strong fingers and slashing out with its terrible weapon. We know that it hunted in packs, since large numbers have been found together, and with the great claw it could have ripped up and killed the largest plant-eaters of the Lower Cretaceous. This animal's name was *Deinonychus*.

Since this discovery, several other related dinosaurs have been found in North America and eastern Asia.

52

Were any of the dinosaurs intelligent?

We usually think of dinosaurs as slow stupid creatures, and indeed many of them were. Many of the big plant-eaters had brains the size of a walnut to control a body the size of a railway engine. However, the coelurosaurs were different. Many of them had very large brains compared with other reptiles.

Saurornithoides was one particularly brainy dinosaur. It was one of the sickle-clawed dinosaurs, but its sickle claw was not as well developed as that of *Deinonychus*. It lived in eastern Asia during the Upper Cretaceous and may have hunted the plant-eating reptiles and early mammals living in the mountains there. The most noticeable feature of its skull is the large eye sockets. They were arranged so that the animal could focus on a single point in front of it, just as our eyes do. This must have been a great help in hunting. The large eyes may mean that it hunted at night or in the late evening or early morning. Its arms were much longer than those of its relatives and this may mean that it hunted small animals in cracks and crevices.

When palaeontologists measured the brain cavity in the skull they found that *Saurornithoides* must have been about six times as intelligent as a crocodile of the same size. Even though crocodiles are not very intelligent, this is still a remarkable figure for a dinosaur. Some palaeontologists have even suggested that if the dinosaurs had survived to the present day, a descendant of *Saurornithoides* may have become as intelligent as a human being!

Saurornithoides, *the intelligent hunter from Upper Cretaceous Mongolia*

Ornithosuchus, *an advanced thecodont or the first carnosaur?*

What is a carnosaur?

As we have already seen, the meat-eating dinosaurs are divided into two separate lines. The first line consists of the small, lightly-built coelurosaurs. The second consists of the big, slower-moving carnosaurs.

Like the coelurosaurs, the carnosaurs evolved in Triassic times, probably from the same ancestors. With plenty of large plant-eating animals around there was enough food for large meat-eaters and they quickly evolved into quite huge sizes. *Teratosaurus* was a 6-metre (20-feet) long hunter from the Upper Triassic of Germany. It gave rise to *Megalosaurus* – a well-known Upper Jurassic dinosaur from southern England. *Megalosaurus* was the first dinosaur to have been discovered and described back in 1822.

Megalosaurus has always been regarded as the typical meat-eating dinosaur. It walked on two legs, holding its body horizontal, balanced by a long tail. It had long hind legs with three-toed feet but its forelimbs were short. It had three clawed fingers on each hand to hold its prey, and saw-edged teeth to tear off chunks of meat. Most carnosaurs followed this pattern.

When did carnosaurs evolve?

We have seen that the meat-eating dinosaurs were the first dinosaurs, and they evolved sometime in the Triassic period. However, as with all other types of animals, we cannot tell for sure where the ancestral line ends and the dinosaur line begins.

Most palaeontologists regard *Ornithosuchus* as the first of the carnosaurs. However, many think of this creature as a very advanced thecodont. It looked very much like a crocodile that had pulled itself up on to its hind legs so that it could move quickly. Its back was covered in bony scales, just like a crocodile, and down the centre these formed a ridge, with spines sticking out of the back of the neck. It grew to a length of about 3.5 metres (12 feet) and its forelimbs were slightly shorter than its hind. Its feet had five toes but it probably only ran on three of them, and its hands had five fingers.

Fossils of *Ornithosuchus* lie in Upper Triassic sandstones of northern Scotland. This area was upland desert at the time, and the creature probably preyed on the other small reptiles that lived there during this period. It had a gland on its face that oozed out any surplus salt that had gathered in its body – something that many desert animals possess.

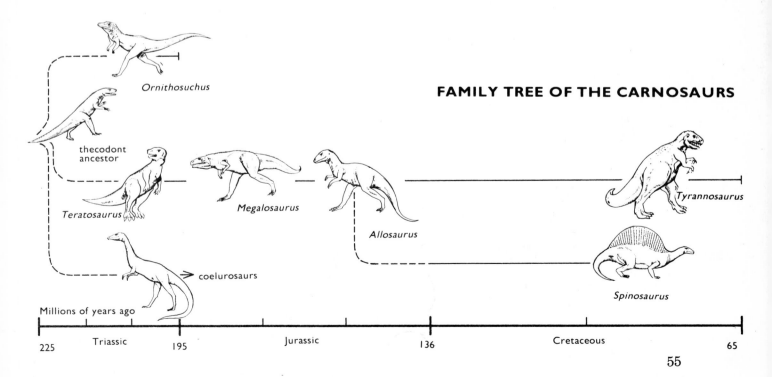

FAMILY TREE OF THE CARNOSAURS

Ornithosuchus

thecodont ancestor

Teratosaurus

Megalosaurus

Allosaurus

Tyrannosaurus

Spinosaurus

coelurosaurs

Millions of years ago

| 225 | Triassic | 195 | Jurassic | 136 | Cretaceous | 65 |

Which were the biggest Jurassic meat-eaters?

Two Allosaurus *attack an* Apatosaurus *on the banks of a sluggish jungle river in what is now Colorado*

In Upper Jurassic times a broad shallow sea spread southwards through North America, covering much of the area of the Mid-West. Further west the young Rocky Mountains were already in existence. The streams and rivers tumbled off the mountains and meandered lazily across flat jungle plains towards the sea. The river gravels and sands deposited in this area now lie as sandstones across the states of Utah, Colorado and New Mexico. Geologists call these rocks the Morrison Formation as they were first studied in a town called Morrison in Colorado.

Amongst these swamps and forests lived some of the best known of the dinosaurs. Huge sauropods lived by the banks of the rivers and

lakes, and they were preyed upon by very large carnosaurs. One of the biggest of the time was *Allosaurus*, 11 metres (36 feet) long and weighing 2 tonnes. Some palaeontologists think that *Allosaurus* was a hunter, while others think it was a scavenger and only ate the bodies of sauropods that had died by accident or of old age. In either case, we know that it fed on them, since we have found fossils of sauropod bones that have been chewed and mangled by *Allosaurus* teeth. What is more, broken *Allosaurus* teeth lie all round such dramatic remains.

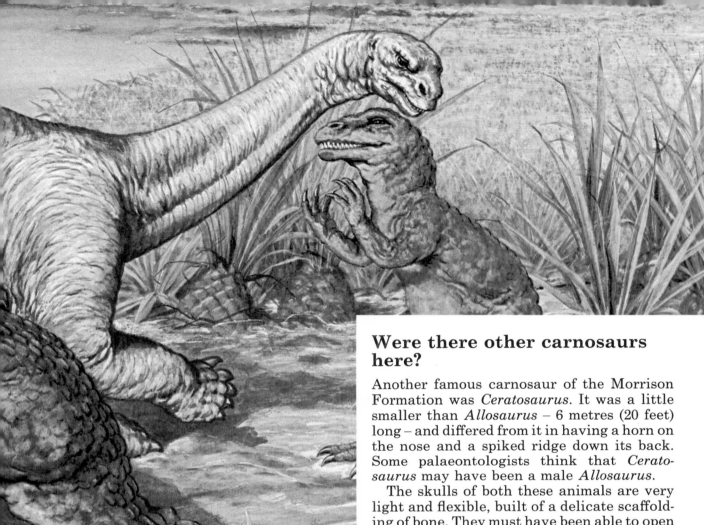

Were there other carnosaurs here?

Another famous carnosaur of the Morrison Formation was *Ceratosaurus*. It was a little smaller than *Allosaurus* – 6 metres (20 feet) long – and differed from it in having a horn on the nose and a spiked ridge down its back. Some palaeontologists think that *Ceratosaurus* may have been a male *Allosaurus*.

The skulls of both these animals are very light and flexible, built of a delicate scaffolding of bone. They must have been able to open their jaws very wide to swallow great chunks of meat.

Ceratosaurus. *Tracks of this dinosuaur run in groups across the sandbanks of the Morrison Formation. This suggests that they hunted or scavenged in groups*

Spinosaurus, *the 12 m (39 ft) long sail-backed carnosaur from north Africa*

Were there desert-living carnosaurs?

Most of the carnosaurs we have seen up to now lived in forests, swamps and jungles. However, during the Cretaceous, there were some that lived at the edges of deserts in what is now North Africa.

Spinosaurus was such a dinosaur. The shape of its body was very much like the big carnosaurs that we have already seen, although the forelimbs were fairly large for a meat-eating dinosaur. Its skull was very similar to that of other carnosaurs, except that the teeth were straight rather than curved. However, the big difference was that it sported a sail down its back, like that of the pelycosaurs of Permian times. The sail was supported on long spines of bone that grew from the vertebrae.

Spinosaurus probably used the sail in the same way as the pelycosaurs used theirs – to control the body temperature. In the morning it would have sat sideways to the rising sun, letting the sun's warmth seep into the sail. It could then become warm and active long before the other cold-blooded animals in the area. It would then go hunting while its prey was still cold and sluggish. At midday if it got too hot it could sit with its sail to the wind and cool off.

How complete is our knowledge?

Palaeontologists have found a number of entire carnosaur skeletons and so our knowledge of these is quite complete. However, most of the skeletons discovered are broken up. All we find are scattered bones, and it is impossible to tell what kind of animal they came from. Sometimes palaeontologists can tell that these are carnosaur bones but that is all. The other groups of dinosaur also have their mystery members.

As we have seen, a dinosaur's skull – and particularly a carnosaur's skull – was very delicate and lightly-built. This means that it was hardly ever fossilized. A great many dinosaur skeletons are complete except for the head.

Dilophosaurus is a particularly interesting case. Its skeleton looked like that of a perfectly normal megalosaur, except that there were two bony blades lying beside the skull. Nobody understood these and most palaeontologists thought that they must have come from a different animal. Eventually a complete skull was found that showed that the bony blades were attached to the animal's head. We still do not know what they were used for but we now know what *Dilophosaurus* looked like.

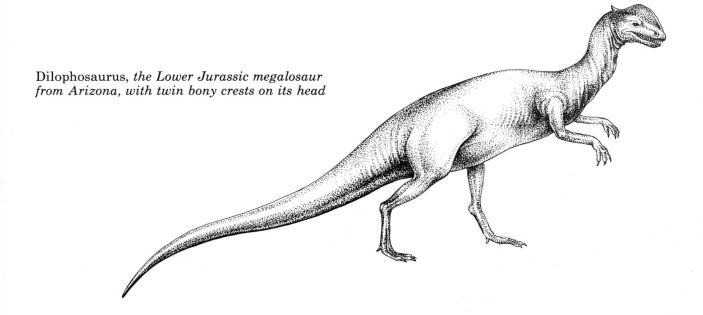

Dilophosaurus, *the Lower Jurassic megalosaur from Arizona, with twin bony crests on its head*

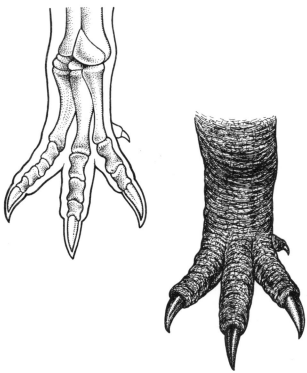

The foot of an advanced carnosaur and coelurosaur had three main toes which took the animal's weight, and usually another toe that did not reach the ground

What were the feet like?

Palaeontologists regard the foot bones of the meat-eating dinosaurs as being similar to those of a mammal. This applies both to the coelurosaurs and the carnosaurs. Hence the meat-eaters are together known as the theropods – the beast-footed dinosaurs. This distinguished them from the sauropods – the lizard-footed members of the lizard-hipped dinosaurs. Confusing isn't it?

What were carnosaur arms like?

It would appear that carnosaurs did not have much use for their forelimbs. We have seen that as the meat-eaters evolved through the Triassic, Jurassic and Cretaceous periods, their arms became smaller and smaller. Not only that, but their fingers became fewer and fewer. In Triassic times, *Ornithosuchus* had five fingers on each hand. The biggest carnosaurs at the end of the Cretaceous had tiny little arms, with only two fingers.

These tiny limbs must have been almost useless. They certainly could not have been used for killing or tearing at flesh. Their only function may have been to stop the dinosaur from sliding forward on to its nose as it raised itself from the ground.

Of course there are exceptions to every rule. In Upper Cretaceous rocks of eastern Asia, palaeontologists found a pair of arms from a meat-eating dinosaur. And these arms were 2.5 metres (8 feet) long! They ended in three huge claws that must have made fearsome weapons. No other bones of this animal have been found, and so no one knows if the body was as huge. We do not even know if the beast was a coelurosaur or a carnosaur. It has been given the name *Deinocheirus* – meaning terrible hand. And terrible hand it must have been too, with such enormous arms and huge sharp claws. It would have made short work of any hapless plant-eating animal that got in its way.

The huge arm bones of Deinocheirus, *the only part of the animal that we know*

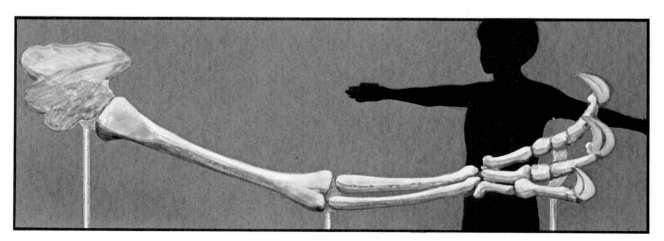

Albertosaurus, *one of the big carrion-eating carnosaurs*

How did the big carnosaurs live?

Some of the biggest flesh-eaters of all time lived in the Upper Cretaceous. There were many different types including *Albertosaurus* and *Daspletosaurs* from North America and *Tarbosaurus* from Asia. These were all very large animals weighing up to 6 tonnes, with huge heads and teeth like steak knives, but with tiny two-fingered arms. The shape of the hips and the length of stride measured on their footprints shows that they were pretty slow movers. They could not have moved at more than about 8 kilometres (5 miles) per hour, and must have had a waddling gait – swinging the body from side to side balanced by the stiff tail. Such an animal could not have run down and killed its prey, so it seems likely that these big meat-eaters were not hunters but were merely scavengers, eating the dead bodies of other creatures, or feasting on the remains of another hunter's kill.

Albertosaurus *rising after a meal, using its tiny arms to prevent it from sliding along the ground*

Which was the biggest carnosaur?

We always think of the biggest meat-eater as being *Tyrannosaurus*. It was a relative of *Albertosaurus*, *Daspletosaurus* and *Tarbosaurus*, but was much bigger than all of these.

It reached a length of about 12 metres (39 feet) and weighed over 6 tonnes. In its metre-(3-feet) long jaws were rows of saw-edged teeth 180 millimetres (7 inches) long. However, despite its ferocious appearance it would have been a scavenger, like its relatives. The fierce teeth would have easily broken in a fight with another animal.

Tyrannosaurus lived at the very end of the Cretaceous period in North America. It must have been one of the last of the dinosaurs.

Why is it often called *Tyrannosaurus rex*?

When scientists give a name to an animal, or a plant, the name is in two parts, the first part is the genus name and the second is the species name. Your scientific name is *Homo sapiens* – you belong to the genus *Homo* and the species *sapiens*. This will distinguish you from your early ancestors such as *Homo habilis* or *Homo erectus*.

All the dinosaurs have genus and species names as well so we should really be talking about *Albertosaurus sternbergi*, *Spinosaurus aegypticus* or *Deinonychus antirrhopus*. However, it would be very difficult to tell one species of *Albertosaurus* from another, and there is many a genus of dinosaur that has only one species. Hence we very rarely use a dinosaur's full scientific name.

In the case of *Tyrannosaurus* the species name of the most well-known one is *rex*, meaning king. As we always seem to think of *Tyrannosaurus* as being the biggest and most majestic of the meat-eaters its full scientific name, *Tyrannosaurus rex*, seems quite appropriate. That is why it is often given in books that ignore the full scientific names of the other dinosaurs.

How big were the meat-eaters?

It is difficult to imagine the size of a huge animal when it is given in mere figures. The illustration below gives some idea of the sizes of the largest carnosaurs when compared to yourself.

You would hardly have reached the knee of a *Tyrannosaurus*! The spines that supported the sail of *Spinosaurus* would have been as tall as you! Even the early *Teratosaurus* from the Triassic would have towered to twice your height! Yet even these great creatures will appear quite small when we look at the animals that they ate.

The sizes of three carnosaurs compared with a human being

Teratosaurus

Tyrannosaurus

Spinosaurus

Tyrannosaurus rex, *the king of the meat-eaters*

Brachiosaurus, *a typical sauropod*

What is a sauropod?

As we have seen, the lizard-hipped dinosaurs – the saurischia – were divided into two separate groups. There were the meat-eaters – the coelurosaurs and the carnosaurs which together we call the theropods – and there was a group of plant-eaters. The plant-eaters all had large bodies, long necks, elephant-like legs and small heads. We call this group the sauropods.

The sauropods were a very successful dinosaur group. They evolved in the Triassic period and continued until the very end of the age of dinosaurs at the top of the Cretaceous. The group contained both the smallest and the largest of the dinosaurs, and one of these may have been the largest land animal that ever walked the Earth.

How did the sauropods evolve?

The first group to develop were the prosauropods ('pro' means 'before'). They began as meat-eaters like their theropod cousins. Eventually, as the Triassic period wore on, they became plant-eaters. Their bodies became larger at the same time.

By the end of the Triassic the prosauropods had died out, but not before a descendant of one of them had evolved into the first sauropod proper. Many different sauropod groups developed in the Jurassic period. Soon they were the most important plant-eaters on land. They survived into the Cretaceous, some continued to the very end.

FAMILY TREE OF THE SAUROPODS

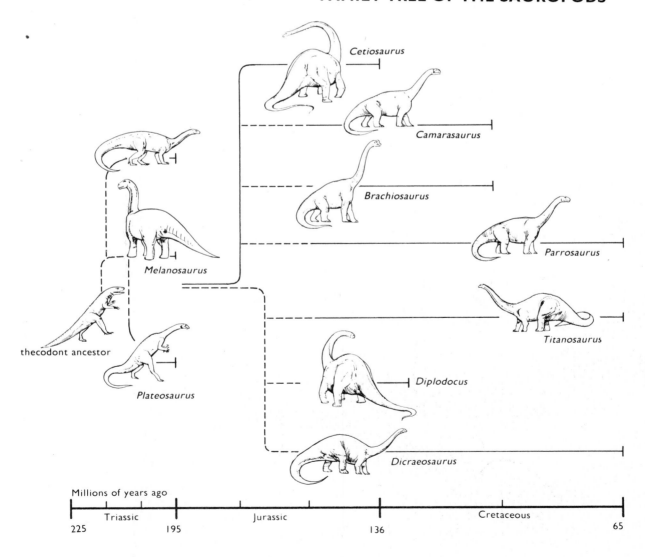

Cetiosaurus

Camarasaurus

Brachiosaurus

Parrosaurus

Melanosaurus

Titanosaurus

thecodont ancestor

Plateosaurus

Diplodocus

Dicraeosaurus

Millions of years ago

Triassic   Jurassic   Cretaceous

225   195   136   65

Why are they called sauropods?

Sauropod means, literally, 'lizard-footed'. The term refers to the bones of the foot. Palaeontologists see these as being similar to the bones in the foot of a lizard.

To us a sauropod's foot would look more like the foot of an elephant. It would have to be – to support the weight of the biggest animal on Earth! It had five toes and they all reached the ground – unlike the very specialized feet of the theropods. On the hind feet there were three very large claws. These helped the animal to grip in the mud. Many skeletons in museums have three large claws on the forefeet as well. This is because in a famous skeleton of *Diplodocus* (see page 72), the bones of the front feet were missing when it was discovered. The palaeontologists assumed that the front feet would have been the same as the back and gave them three claws as well. It was not until recently that the front feet of *Diplodocus* were found, and these only had a large claw on one toe.

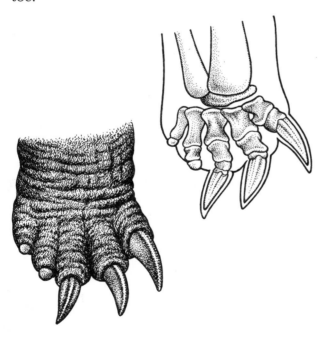

The hind foot of a sauropod showing big claws on three of the toes, and little hooves on the others

How were sauropods built?

If you had to build a house with different-sized bricks and different types of material, how would you go about it? You would probably put the biggest and strongest bricks at the bottom to take the weight and build the higher parts of lighter materials. A sauropod's skeleton was built exactly like that.

The legs were huge, made of heavy compact bones. They acted as the foundations for the whole structure. The feet were broad, to hold the weight of the great body and spread it over as large an area as possible.

The backbone, on the other hand, was built of lightweight bone. Each vertebra was a kind of scaffolding, giving as much strength as possible with very little weight. Long spines jutted upwards from each vertebra and these held tendons – strong flexible straps lashing the vertebrae together and helping to keep the neck and the tail stretched out. This whole arrangement was firmly fixed to the limbs by long shoulder blades and broad hip bones. All these features can be seen in the drawing on page 16.

As for the rest of the skeleton, a huge rib-cage made the body barrel-like and held all the internal organs. The hip bones were the typical saurischian type – with the front bones jutting forward, keeping the internal organs forward of the hind legs.

There were different kinds of sauropod skull, but most had narrow, peg-like teeth.

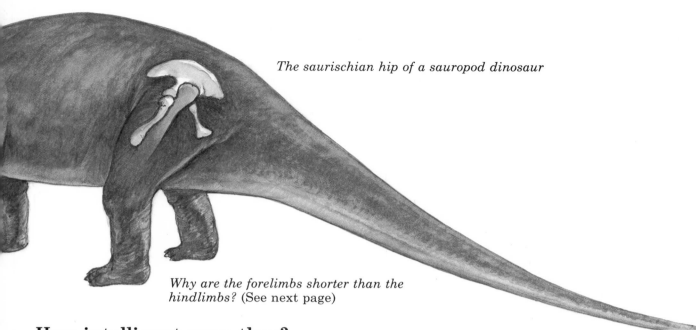

The saurischian hip of a sauropod dinosaur

Why are the forelimbs shorter than the hindlimbs? (See next page)

How intelligent were they?

Sauropods were stupid. That is the only conclusion that we can come to. Many had a brain about the size of that of a kitten. This was housed in a skull the size of that of a horse. And it had to control a body as big as that of a whale! Many of the bodily functions that we take for granted must have been very slow to operate in a sauropod dinosaur. Either that or they were non-existent.

For example, if the tip of a sauropod's tail was attacked by a marauding carnosaur, it may have been several seconds before it felt any pain. Then, when the brain knew that it was being attacked, it would have taken several more seconds to react to the danger.

By that time the poor creature could have suffered terrible damage. It may even be that a sauropod could not feel pain at all, something as complicated as pain being beyond the powers of its tiny brain.

However, the weak brain may have had help from elsewhere. In the hips, in the area that the spinal cord passes through, there is a large cavity. This cavity may have held an extra nerve-centre. Such a nerve-centre would not have worked like an extra brain, but it may have helped to control the nerves of the tail and the hind legs.

Some palaeontologists disagree with this. They say that the cavity held a gland that supplied extra energy to the legs and tail.

A nerve-centre in the base of the tail may have helped to control the nerves through the massive body of a sauropod

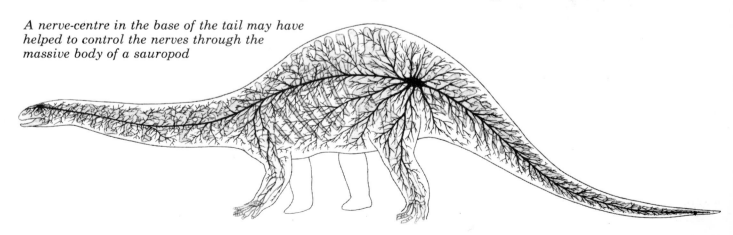

What were the sauropod ancestors like?

The early dinosaur group that evolved into the sauropods are called the prosauropods. They lived in the Triassic period and evolved from the same creatures as the early theropods. Like the theropods, the prosauropods ate meat. We can see that by looking at their teeth, which were sharp and pointed. However, as time went on they turned to a diet that consisted mostly of plants. Their bodies became big and their necks became long, but their heads remained fairly small.

Their plant-eating diet meant that they needed a large volume of intestine. They would have needed this to break down the tough fibres of the leaves and stems that they ate. Hence the development of the huge body. Because of the shape of the hips the intestine had to be carried well forward of the hind legs, and so the prosauropods had to go down on to all fours to balance.

The feet all had five toes. They became broad to take the weight of the big body. There was a long claw on the thumb, just like the single claw on a sauropod's forefoot. This would have been used to pull down leaves and branches as the animal reared up to reach its food. The prosauropods developed strong hind legs and tail to help them swim. They had short forelimbs – just like their thecodont ancestors – but they never became as short as theropods' forelimbs.

Skull of a prosauropod. Note the small pointed teeth

How big were they?

Most prosauropods were fairly small for dinosaurs. Two to 3 metres (7 to 10 feet) was a good length for them. However, some became considerably larger. *Melanosaurus* from the Upper Triassic of South Africa was about 12 metres (39 feet) long. This is about the size of a fully-developed sauropod and so some palaeontologists think that *Melanosaurus* was really the first sauropod. However, footprints of a true sauropod have been found in the same rock as *Melanosaurus*, so the sauropods had already evolved by the time *Melanosaurus* was around.

Plateosaurus, *a typical prosauropod about 6 m (20 ft) long from the Upper Triassic of Germany*

How did they live?

The prosauropods lived in the Triassic period. As we have seen this was a time of deserts and mountains. There would probably have been plenty of food for them in oases, in moist mountain valleys and by the seas.

Plateosaurus was a typical prosauropod from Germany. We know from its remains that it lived in herds and that these herds migrated from time to time across the deserts. The Tethys Sea, at this time, reached into southern Germany, and there were hilly areas to the north. We think that the *Plateosaurus* herds spent most of the time in the wooded valleys of the hilly area and, in the dry season, they migrated across the deserts towards the sea in the south. Many of them died on the way and their skeletons lie fossilized in the German desert sandstones.

Where did they live?

Prosauropod remains have been found all over the world. Those that lived in Europe are almost identical to those that lived in North America. Even more significantly, the huge *Melanosaurus* of South Africa is very similar to another enormous form, *Riojasaurus*, from South America. All the continents were crammed together in one great super-continent at that time (see page 37).

Apatosaurus, *the typical sauropod*

70

Palaeontologists used to think that Apatosaurus *had a short head, like those on the left. We now know that the head was long, like that on the right*

What was its head like?

Until recently all restorations of *Apatosaurus* had a head that was chunky and box-like. In fact, this was pure guesswork. *Apatosaurus* skeletons are quite common but they always lack the head. A dinosaur's skull is very fragile so it is often lost. A famous skeleton in the American Museum of Natural History in New York has the box-like skull of another sauropod placed upon it. Only in 1979 was an *Apatosaurus* skull discovered, and this proved to be long and narrow, like that of *Diplodocus*.

Why is it sometimes called *Brontosaurus*?

Often a palaeontologist will find part of a fossil animal and give it a scientific name. Later, he or she might find that it is part of an animal that has already been discovered by another palaeontologist, and given a different name. When this happens the rule is that we accept the first name given.

That is what happened to *Apatosaurus*. It was discovered and named. Later, someone else discoverd more skeletons and named them *Brontosaurus*, meaning 'thunder lizard'. This name seemed so appropriate that it stuck. It was only recently that the two names were found to belong to the same animal and so the earlier name had to be adopted. Its full scientific name is *Apatosaurus ajax*.

Which is the best-known sauropod?

Apatosaurus probably fits everybody's idea of what a sauropod dinosaur looked like. It was about 21 metres (70 feet) long and its body was 4.5 metres (15 feet high) at the shoulder. It must have weighed about 30 tonnes. It lived in the swamps, rivers and forests of the Upper Jurassic Morrison Formation of North America. There was certainly enough vegetation in the area to support herds of the creatures. With its tiny head and long neck *Apatosaurus* must have spent all day just eating so that it could gain enough nourishment to keep its great body going.

Like the other sauropods, *Apatosaurus'* massive body was supported on elephantine legs. It had a long snaky neck and a long tail. Its front legs were shorter than the hind, so the body sloped down from the hips to the shoulders. It is the animal that most of us think about immediately when the word dinosaur is mentioned.

Which was the longest sauropod?

There were many different sauropods living amongst the forests and swamps of the Morrison Formation. One of the most well known was *Diplodocus*. It may not have been the longest but it was certainly very long. It reached a length of 27 metres (88.5 feet). Eight metres (26 feet) of this consisted of neck. The body was 4 metres (13 feet) long. The long whip-like tail made up the rest of the length. For all its great length it was very lightly-built, and may have weighed no more than 10 tonnes.

The name 'diplodocus' means 'double-beam' and this refers to the bones of the tail. Each tail vertebra had a pair of skids that protruded downwards. These protected the muscles and the blood-vessels of the tail as it dragged on the ground.

The skull was long and narrow, with the nostrils on the top. The teeth were thin and peg-like and arranged like a comb. These were probably used to strain water weed from the muddy waters of the swamps in which it lived. They may also have been used to comb the leaves from branches and twigs.

Diplodocus lived in North America and in England during the Upper Jurassic.

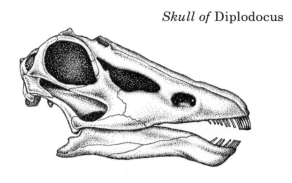

Skull of Diplodocus

Why is it so well-known

Diplodocus was first discoverd in 1902 by an expedition financed by millionaire Andrew Carnegie. He was so impressed by it that he had casts made of all 300 bones of the skeleton and donated them to museums all around the world. You can now see casts of this *Diplodocus* skeleton in London, Pittsburgh, Frankfurt, Paris, Berlin, Bologna, Vienna and La Plata.

Because of Carnegie's generous actions, the scientific name given to this animal is *Diplodocus carnegii*.

Diplodocus

Camarasaurus

Were there any large-headed sauropods?

Another important group of the sauropods was the one to which *Camarasaurus* belonged. This group lived in Upper Jurassic and Lower Cretaceous times. Palaeontologists have found their fossils in North America, Europe and Asia. In 1972 they found bones that may belong to an animal of this group in Lower Jurassic rocks in Africa.

Camarasaurus itself must have been about 18 metres (59 feet) long, but the best-known skeleton is of a 5-metre (16-feet) youngster from the Morrison Formation of Utah. An adult *Camarasaurus* would have looked quite different from the other sauropods. The neck and tail were shorter – much shorter than those of *Diplodocus* – and the head was large and box-like.

A relative of *Camarasaurus*, called *Cetiosaurus*, was one of the first dinosaurs to be discovered – but nobody knew it at the time! When the bones were first found in England in 1809 the palaeontologists thought that they belonged to a whale. It was only when complete sauropod skeletons were discovered in the Morrison Formation that they realized that these British bones were from a dinosaur. Its full scientific name is *Cetiosaurus oxoniensis* – *Cetiosaurus* meaning 'whale lizard' and *oxoniensis* after Oxford, where it was found.

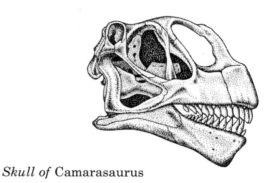

Skull of Camarasaurus

What was a *Camarasaurus* skull like?

The skull of *Camarasaurus* was quite different from that of *Diplodocus*. It was square and box-like, but lightly-built with very large nostril openings. The teeth were strong and spoon-shaped, and arranged all along the jaws – not just at the front.

Different palaeontologists have different ideas of why the nostril openings are so large. One explanation is that the big, moist nostril area could keep the inside of the head cool. This would prevent the little brain from overheating in warm weather. Another explanation is that the head had a trunk, like an elephant's. However, it is difficult to imagine why the creature would need a trunk – it already had a long neck.

Which were the tallest dinosaurs?

One group of sauropods were very much taller than all the rest. *Brachiosaurus* belonged to this group. It differed from the other sauropods in that its forelimbs were longer than the hind. This meant that the body sloped upwards from the hips to the shoulders, and provided a strong base for the tall neck.

The most famous skeleton of *Brachiosaurus* is in Berlin. This is 23 metres (75 feet) long – almost as long as *Diplodocus*. However, where *Diplodocus* was long and low, *Brachiosaurus* was tall. The head of the Berlin skeleton towers 12 metres (39 feet) above the visitors to the museum!

The skull is very much like that of *Camarasaurus*. The framework of bone surrounding the nostrils is tall and projects up above the eyes. The nostril openings must have been at the top of the head. Or else, as some palaeontologists suggest, the animal had a trunk like that of an elephant. The jaws are longer than those of *Camarasaurus* and stick out in front of the rest of the skull. The teeth are quite long and sturdy – more like the teeth of *Camarasaurus* than those of *Diplodocus*.

How did the brachiosaurs live?

When we look at pictues of the Berlin *Brachiosaurus* reconstruction, or restorations of the dinosaur in the same vertical-necked position, the neck and head look just like a periscope or snorkel. This led to an early idea that *Brachiosaurus* lived deep underwater, in rivers or lakes, with only the head – or even just the nostrils – breaking the surface. We do not think that this is likely any more, since the water pressure at that depth would be so great that the animal would not have been able to breathe.

Brachiosaurus

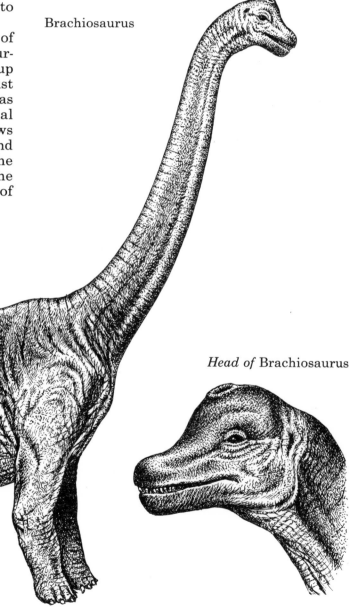

Head of Brachiosaurus

Another suggestion is that *Brachiosaurus* was a land-living animal and existed like a giraffe. It could have used its long neck to reach the leaves and twigs from the tops of trees.

A third suggestion is that they lived shoulder-deep in the water. From this position they could have swept around them with their long necks, gathering up floating waterweed from a wide area.

Did Brachiosaurus *live in deep water, in shallow water or on land?*

Where did they live?

The first *Brachiosaurus* fossils were found in 1900 in the Morrison Formation of Colorado – just like many other sauropods. However, the skeleton that now stands in Berlin is from Tanzania. In the early years of this century Tanzania was part of the German empire and called German East Africa. The conditions in that part of Africa during the Upper Jurassic were just like those in North America. Many animals were also the same. The continents were still all joined together at that time.

Which was the biggest dinosaur?

The biggest dinosaur for which we have a complete skeleton is *Brachiosaurus*. However, this is not the biggest that ever lived. In 1972 palaeontologists discovered a shoulder blade and some vertebrae of a brachiosaur in Colorado. These were enormous and must have come from an animal 30 metres (98 feet) long, 15 metres (49 feet) high and weighing about 100 tonnes. So far the animal has not been given a scientific name but its nickname is 'Supersaurus'.

The discoveries did not stop there. Not far away the palaeontologists found more bones of something even bigger. This brachiosaur may have weighed about 130 tonnes. Its nickname is 'Ultrasaurus'.

There is more, indirect, evidence of truly enormous animals. There are fossil footprints in Upper Jurassic rocks in Morocco that must have been made by an animal 48 metres (157 feet) long! Without doubt the biggest land animals the world has ever known were the brachiosaurs.

Which was the smallest dinosaur?

The smallest dinosaur skeleton that we have so far discovered is of a tiny little prosauropod that was only 20 centimetres (8 inches) long. It is called *Mussaurus* meaning 'mouse lizard'. Palaeontologists found it in Upper Triassic rocks of Argentina. However it was a very young dinosaur and still in the nest. The adult may have reached a length of about 3 metres (10 feet).

Mussaurus, *the smallest dinosaur so far discovered*

76

'Ultrasaurus', *the biggest dinosaur so far discovered*

77

How can we tell how sauropods lived?

We can tell a great deal about how any animal lived by looking at its footprints. Something as big and heavy as a sauropod would have left quite large footprints. These have been found as trace fossils in the sandstones of the Morrison Formation and other Jurassic and Cretaceous deposits.

We can see from the tracks that the sauropods lived in herds. If they lived in the water they must have left it from time to time and crossed the mud and the sandbanks. When they did so they travelled in a troupe, with the adults on the outside, protecting the youngsters in the middle. This is the way that elephants travel.

When it was in deep water a sauropod only left the prints of its front feet. This means that it must have floated in the water and pawed its way across the river or lake with its forefeet. Hippopotami do the same thing today. When the animal changed direction it put its hind feet into the mud so that it could swing round. Sometimes it would prod the tip of its tail into the mud to help it to steer.

The sauropod would not have taken to the water to escape carnosaurs. We have found carnosaur footprints in water deposits too.

Sometimes we find polished stones with sauropod skeletons. These are stomach stones and would have been swallowed by the dinosaur to help grind up its food.

They pawed their way across lakes using their front feet . . .

Opposite *Sauropod herds travelled from place to place with their young protected in the middle*

Alamosaurus, *from the Upper Cretaceous of Utah, Texas, Montana and New Mexico. It was one of the last of the sauropods*

What replaced the sauropods as the important plant-eaters of the Cretaceous (See next page)

. . . but carnosaurs could still reach them!

Which were the last sauropods?

The sauropods were the most important plant-eating dinosaurs of the Jurassic period. With the dawn of the Cretaceous they became fewer. By the end of the period there were few left in the northern hemisphere. Those that did survive there were relatives of *Apatosaurus*. The sauropods were still quite common in South America and Africa throughout the Cretaceous. Elsewhere their place as the important plant-eaters was taken by another group – the ornithopods.

79

Fabrosaurus, *the earliest ornithopod*

What is an ornithopod?

The ornithopods were the two-legged, plant-eating dinosaurs. All the dinosaurs we have looked at so far – both meat-eaters and plant-eaters – were lizard-hipped. The ornithopods were the most important group of the bird-hipped dinosaurs.

Most ornithopods were small and lightly-built compared with other plant-eating dinosaurs. They were the browsing animals of the Triassic, Jurassic and Cretaceous periods. They did not defend themselves with horns or armour. Nor did they have the heavy bodies of the sauropods that made them difficult to kill. If danger threatened they would have run away. They were well-suited for that. Most had strong running legs and their bodies would have been well balanced by their stiff tails. In fact, they would have lived very much like the deer and antelope do today.

They evolved in the Triassic and became really important in Cretaceous times.

Which was the earliest?

The earliest ornithopod that we know about is *Fabrosaurus* from the Triassic of southern Africa. It was about 1 metre (3 feet) long. Its legs were long and its limb bones were hollow, showing that it was built for lightness and speed. It had four toes on its hind feet – a primitive feature – and five fingers on its hands. This animal is sometimes called *Lesothosaurus*. The names are given to similar remains in different areas.

It must have lived in quite hot and dry conditions. Many desert animals today curl up and sleep away the harshest summer months. We know that *Fabrosaurus* did this because palaeontologists have found skeletons curled up in their sleeping positions. In their skulls their old teeth had dropped out and new ones had grown in their place. The old ones still lay by the skeletons showing that the animals had been asleep for a long time before they died.

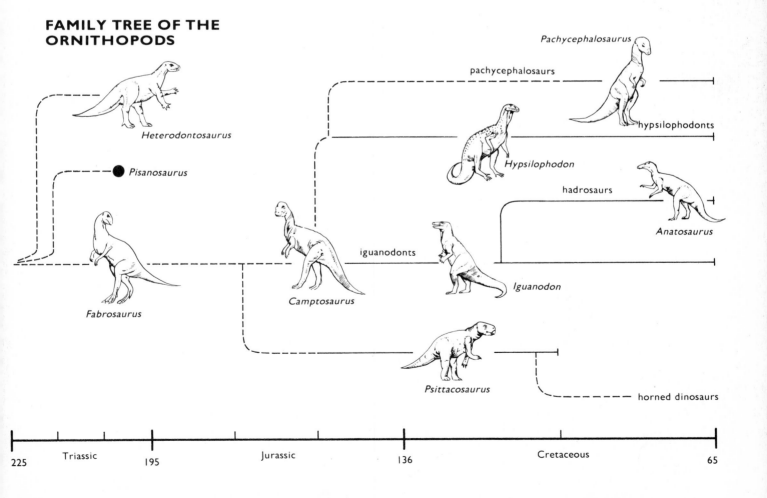

FAMILY TREE OF THE ORNITHOPODS

Heterodontosaurus

Pisanosaurus

Fabrosaurus

Camptosaurus

iguanodonts

Iguanodon

Psittacosaurus

pachycephalosaurs

Pachycephalosaurus

hypsilophodonts

Hypsilophodon

hadrosaurs

Anatosaurus

horned dinosaurs

225   Triassic   195   Jurassic   136   Cretaceous   65

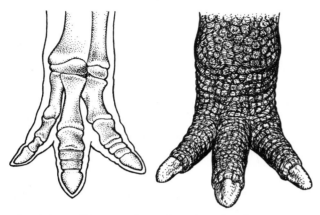

Hind foot of Iguanodon, *showing the three toes and the hooves*

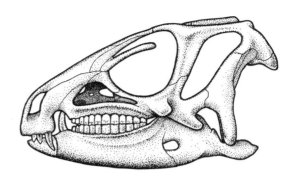

Skull of Heterodontosaurus, *an early ornithopod. Note the tusks. They must have been used for digging up roots*

Why are they called ornithopods?

Fabrosaurus had four toes on each hind foot. Most later ornithopods had only three. These were the middle three – the first and the fifth having been lost. The bones of the toes were arranged like those of a bird. Ornithopod means, literally, 'bird foot'.

On some of the larger ornithopods the toes developed heavy hooves rather than claws. This would have helped to take the weight of a really large animal.

As well as being bird-footed, the ornithopods were also bird-hipped. The bones of the hip were quite different from those of the lizard-hipped theropods and sauropods we have already seen. The bone called the pubis – that sticks forward in the lizard-like hip – sticks back in the bird-like hip. This gives plenty of room for the large intestine that a plant-eating animal needs. In later ornithopods a pair of prepubic bones stick forward above and to the side of the intestines to help to support the body.

Hip bones of an early ornithopod, left, and a later one, right

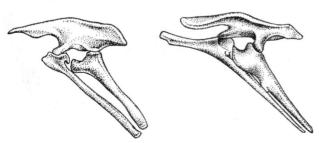

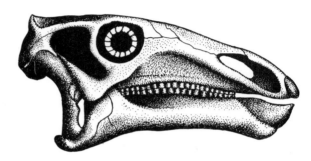

Skull of Iguanodon, *showing the predentary bone at the front of the lower jaw*

What was the ornithopod skull like?

The skull of a bird-hipped dinosaur was open and lightly built, just like most of the other dinosaurs. However, there was an extra bone at the front of the lower jaw. This bone is called the predentary and it did not carry any teeth. Instead it formed a beak. The teeth worked like scissors, snipping and chopping up leaves and twigs.

Most ornithopods had cheek pouches which contained the food as the animal was chewing it. We know this because of the depressions in the sides of the skulls, and also because the scissor action of the teeth would not have worked properly without them. Half of the food would have dropped out of the mouth if there had been no pouches to catch it!

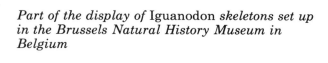

How did ornithopods live?

We have already seen that the smaller ornithopods must have lived like deer or antelopes. But what about the larger ones? About 30 skeletons of *Iguanodon*, one of the largest ornithopods, were found in a coal mine in Belgium in 1878. While they were being assembled in a special display, the then king of Belgium had a look at them. He remarked to the palaeontologist in charge that they looked like a kind of giraffe. He was probably right. *Iguanodon* may well have lived like a giraffe, reaching up to take the juicy leaves from the tops of the trees, and making off in a slow graceful run when danger threatened.

What did the animal look like in life? (See next page)

What did people once think it looked like? (See page 18)

Why should *Iguanodons* be in a coal mine?

Coal was formed in the Carboniferous period about 300 million years ago. *Iguanodons* lived in the Lower Cretaceous and are less than half that age, so why were 30 *Iguanodon* skeletons discovered in a coal mine in Belgium in 1878?

The reason is that during Lower Cretaceous times the Carboniferous rocks existed as a range of hills that stretched from southern England into Belgium. The hills were cut by gullies and ravines which formed as streams flowed down towards the lowlands on each side. Herds of *Iguanodon* lived on these hills, browsing amongst their woods and forests. Palaeontologists think that such a herd blundered into one of these ravines by accident and the *Iguanodons* were all killed.

The herd may have been stampeded by a fierce meat-eater such as *Megalosaurus*, or frightened by a flash of lightning or a forest fire. We do not know. In any case, the bodies piled up in the stream bed and were buried. Ages later the Carboniferous rocks, with their Cretaceous gullies, were buried again and remained like that until Belgian coal miners tunnelled through them.

Where did *Iguanodon* live?

Iguanodon is one of the best-known of the ornithopods. Its skeleton, with its gentle giraffe-like head towering 5 metres (16 feet) above the ground, its hands with the spiky thumbs, its massive hind legs and the long flattened tail, is a familiar sight in museums all over the world. When it was alive the animal must have weighed between 4 and 5 tonnes and reached the impressive length of 9 metres (29.5 feet).

The first *Iguanodon* remains were found in England in the early 19th century and these were followed by the spectacular find in the Belgian coal mine. Since then bones and skeletons have cropped up in North America, southern Europe, north Africa and Asia. Footprints of *Iguanodon*, or something closely related, have been found in several places in South America, and also in Spitzbergen – well inside the Arctic Circle. *Iguanodon* was a truly cosmopolitan dinosaur.

What do we know about *Iguanodon*'s lifestyle?

We can tell by the teeth that *Iguanodon,* and the rest of the ornithopods, ate plants. The teeth were designed for chopping leaves. The front of the mouth formed a kind of beak that was used for snipping off growing plants. It may have had a long tongue like that of a giraffe so it could reach the highest twigs. The thumb was armed with a long spike and this may have been used to slash down branches. It may also have been used to fight off meat-eaters.

Iguanodons lived in herds. We know this because large numbers of footprints have been found together. They lived in the lush wood-lands of the Lower Cretaceous and also prob-ably roamed the marshy lowlands. Some of the marshy deposits of southern England show skin impressions where the great beasts wal-lowed in the mud and grazed the reed-beds of horsetails that flourished there.

Iguanodon was one of the largest, and certainly the best known, of the ornithopods. However, it was by no means the only one. There were many closely related types that were far smaller.

Hypsilophodon looked just like a miniature *Iguanodon* about 2 metres (6.5 feet) long. It was a little more primitive, having four toes on each hind foot. It also had teeth at the front of the upper jaw – something that *Iguanodon* lacked. The legs were particularly long and obviously built for running.

Iguanodon (left), *the big ornithopod of the Lower Cretaceous*

Hypsilophodon (below), *the sprinting ornithopod*

What did palaeontologists once believe about the lifestyle of Hypsilophodon? (See page 19)

Camptosaurus, the primitive ornithopod from the Morrison Formation

Which was the earliest *Iguanodon*?

Iguanodon lived in Lower Cretaceous times. However, it had a close relative that lived in North America and Europe in the Upper Jurassic. Its name was *Camptosaurus*. It looked very much like a small *Iguanodon* about 5 metres (16 feet) long and must have had a similar lifestyle. Some palaeontologists think that *Camptosaurus* was a primitive form of *Iguanodon* while others put it in a group of its own.

The best-known fossils of *Camptosaurus* have been found in the dinosaur-rich Morrison Formation of the Western United States. Many skeletons have been found here ranging in length from about 0.7 metres (2 feet) upwards. The fact that many skeletons lie together suggests that they lived in herds and that the herds consisted of both youngsters and adults.

The forelimbs were fairly large for an ornithopod and three of the fingers of the forelimb had quite heavy hooves on them. This suggests that *Camptosaurus* spent much of its time on all fours. This would have enabled the animal to crop low-growing vegetation, such as the horsetails and ferns that grew by the sides of the rivers.

When startled by a meat-eating dinosaur, *Camptosaurus* would have lifted itself to its hind feet and run off, balancing its body by its stiff tail – just like other two-footed dinosaurs. This is why we often see restorations of *Camptosaurus* in two positions – on all fours and standing up.

The skull was very much like that of an *Iguanodon* with its chopping teeth and its beak, but it was longer and narrower, and had smaller openings in it.

Camptosaurus remains have been found in both North American and European rocks indicating that the two continents were joined together during the Upper Jurassic.

Were there any sail-backed ornithopods?

We have seen that several dinosaurs grew sails down their backs to stay at a constant temperature. The sail consisted of a broad web of skin supported by spines jutting up from the backbone. If the sail was turned towards the sun, the animal would warm up. If it was held into the wind the animal would cool down.

Ouranosaurus was a sail-backed ornithopod. It was about the size of a small *Iguanodon* – about 7 metres (23 feet) long. It looked like an *Iguanodon* too, but had a sloping face and a flattened snout. The big difference, however, was the sail.

Ouranosaurus lived in Lower Cretaceous north Africa. The area was a broad river plain at that time where many meat-eaters lived. These included giant crocodiles, and possibly the sail-backed *Spinosaurus* (see page 59). A heat-regulator would have been useful to keep *Ouranosaurus* active enough to escape them.

Ouranosaurus, *the sail-backed ornithopod from north Africa*

What do we call it, when different animals have the same shapes because they live in the same kind of place? (See page 21)

87

Did any of the ornithopods have armour?

We have seen that most of the ornithopods were quite harmless and inoffensive brutes. They would have run away from a battle rather than stay to fight. Indeed, the light build and long legs of most of them would have given them a good start in any race with a meat-eater.

Nevertheless, there was a group of ornithopods that developed a kind of armour. These were the pachycephalosaurs – the boneheads. To look at, a pachycephalosaur was very much like an *Iguanodon* or a *Camptosaurus* except for the head. The head was very large and dome-shaped, and must have made the animal look very intelligent. But a pachycephalosaur was not particularly intelligent, the dome-shaped head did not contain a very big brain – it was mostly made

Pachycephalosaurus, *the largest of the boneheads*

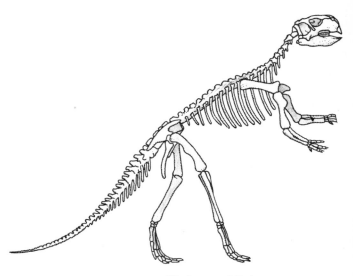

Skeleton of Psittacosaurus

of compact bone. Probably male pachycephalosaurs butted one another with these bony helmets, to see which one was strong enough to be the leader of the herd. Mountain goats do this today.

Pachycephalosaurs lived in hilly areas. Their remains have been found in Upper Cretaceous rocks of North America, Britain, China and even the island of Madagascar in the Indian Ocean. They ranged in size from *Micropachycephalosaurus*, with a length of 50 centimetres (20 inches), to 4.5-metre (15-feet) long *Pachycephalosaurus*.

Psittacosaurus, *the parrot-faced dinosaur*

What did the parrot-faced dinosaurs evolve into? (See page 98)

What other ornithopod oddities were there?

In the Lower Cretaceous rocks of Mongolia the fossils of a small dinosaur called *Psittacosaurus* have been found. It was about 1.5 metres (5 feet) long and, like some of the other ornithopods, it seemed to be as comfortable walking on all fours as walking only on its hind feet. The odd thing about it was its face. The skull was flattened on the sides and ended in a pronounced beak. At its neck the skull had a heavy ridge and altogether the head must have looked very much like that of a parrot. This is the reason for its name; *Psittacosaurus* means 'parrot lizard'.

We can see that it could walk on all fours because the forelimbs were quite large – larger than those of most other ornithopods. It only had four stubby fingers on each hand, suggesting that it did not use its hands much for feeding. The neck was quite long as well, so that it could still look around while it was walking on four legs. Palaeontologists think that *Psittacosaurus*, or something closely related, later evolved into another of the main groups of dinosaurs during the Upper Cretaceous.

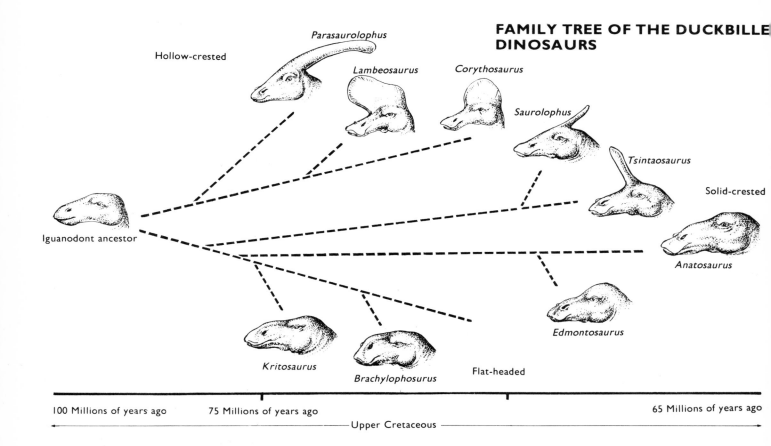

Hollow-crested

Parasaurolophus

Lambeosaurus

Corythosaurus

Saurolophus

Tsintaosaurus

Solid-crested

Iguanodont ancestor

Anatosaurus

Edmontosaurus

Kritosaurus

Brachylophosurus

Flat-headed

100 Millions of years ago   75 Millions of years ago   65 Millions of years ago

— Upper Cretaceous —

What were the Upper Cretaceous ornithopods?

In the second half of the Cretaceous period a particular group of ornithopods developed. These spread and became the most numerous and varied dinosaur family that ever lived. They were the hadrosaurs. They are better known as the duckbills because of the shape of the face. The front of the snout and the predentary bone (see page 82) on the lower jaw were expanded into a flat, duck-like bill that was used for cropping vegetation. The duckbills lasted to the very end of the age of dinosaurs. They were so successful that in some places three dinosaurs out of every four were duckbills at that time.

How did the duckbills develop?

The earliest duckbills have been found in Lower Cretaceous rocks in Mongolia. Palaeontologists think that this is where they originated. From there they spread both east and west – into Europe and North America. Asia and North America were joined together at this time. They were very successful in North America where they almost completely replaced the big sauropods as the main browsers of the swamp forests. They reached South America as well but were never really successful. It may be that South America separated from North America at about this time and the duckbills did not have a real chance to take over there. Sauropods thrived until the end of the Cretaceous in South America. No duckbills reached Africa, India or Australia. These continents had broken away from the main landmass by the Upper Cretaceous.

At a very early stage the duckbills divided into two main lines. One line consisted of those with a hollow crest on their skulls. The other line consisted of those with no crests, or with crests of solid bone. Apart from these marked differences in the skulls, one duckbill was very much like another. The body was like that of *Iguanodon* – the duckbills were descended from the *Iguanodon* group. It was balanced by a heavy tail that was flattened on the sides. There were three toes on the hind feet and four stubby fingers on each hand.

How did duckbills live?

The name 'duckbill' suggests that these animals lived rather like ducks. That may well have been the case. Their shovel-like snouts would have been fine for raking up waterweed. Their forelimbs had webbed fingers, suggesting that they spent at least some time in the water. The deeply flattened tail would have made a powerful swimming organ – just like a crocodile's.

However, it is unlikely that the duckbills spent a lot of time in the water. Their main food seems to have been conifer needles browsed from the riverside forests. Their tightly-packed, grinding cheek teeth were built for tough stuff like this, rather than for soft waterweed. Possibly they browsed in the forests in herds and took to the water when danger threatened.

We know that they had a complicated family life. Palaeontologists have found duckbill nests – great mounds of mud 3 metres (10 feet) in diameter and 1.5 metres (5 feet) high. Youngsters in these nests must have been looked after by their parents for a long time after they had hatched. We know this because we have found the remains of 11 youngsters inside one of the nests. These youngsters were not hatchlings – they were

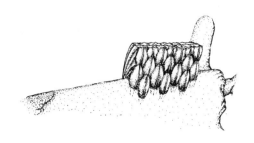

A hadrosaur's grinding teeth. See how tightly-packed they are

about 1 metre (3 feet) in length, which is quite grown up for this type of dinosaur. Several of these nests were found close together which suggests that the hadrosaurs lived in 'rookeries' like many seabirds today. The advantage of this is that while some adults were out foraging, the whole nest site could be defended by those left at home. The name given to the actual hadrosaur that made the nest is *Maiasaura*, which means 'good mother lizard'. It was one of the solid-crested type, and reached a respectable adult length of about 9 metres (30 feet). Since this discovery was made in 1979 we have found evidence that other dinosaur types also had structured family lives.

A typical duckbill walking at speed. Its body would have been held forward, balanced by the tail

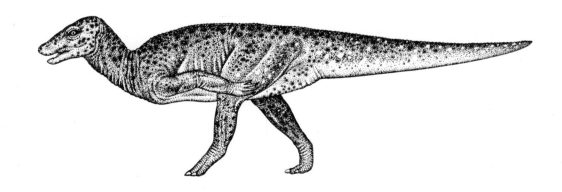

What were the duckbills' crests?

The crest on the skull of a hollow-crested duckbill was entirely made up of the nose bones. The nasal passages went from the nostrils, right back into the crest, usually along a very twisted path, and descended into the top of the skull and then down into the neck towards the lungs. The crest itself was either a deep wall-like structure, as in *Corythosaurus* or *Lambeosaurus*, or else it formed a long curved spike, as in *Parasaurolophus*.

In *Parasaurolophus* the nasal passage swept straight back from the snout to the tip of the crest, and doubled straight back again. In the deeper-crested forms the nasal passage reached the same kind of length by being curled up and folded inside the smaller crest. Many types of crested duckbill existed, each one had its own kind of skull ornament.

Parasaurolophus, *one of the most spectacular of the hollow-crested duckbills*

The crest of Corythosaurus *was larger in the male than in the female or the young*

Young   Female   Male

What was the purpose of the crests?

That is a question that many, many palaeontologists have asked. They have come up with many, many answers – some more likely than others.

Because the crest of the hollow-crested duckbills contained the nasal passages, an early idea was that the duckbills could use them as some sort of an aqualung or snorkel while feeding underwater. This is not very likely. There are more believable explanations.

It could be that the large wet area inside the nasal passage could have acted as a cooling device, carrying heat away from the brain during hot spells in the open.

Possibly a large distinctive crest helped a duckbill to recognize a herd of its own species. Maybe it was a display structure used in courtship. Certainly the crest of a male *Corythosaurus* was much larger than that of a female or a young one. An interesting suggestion is that the nasal passage acted as the resonating chamber in a musical instrument, enabling duckbills to bellow at one another across the swamps.

What about the solid-crested duckbills?

The hollow-crested duckbills could have used their crests to cool their brains, or to trumpet to one another through the forests and across the plains, or increase their sense of smell, or even all three. But the solid-crested forms such as *Saurolophus* or *Tsintaosaurus* could have done none of these things.

It looks as if a solid crest could only have been used as some sort of display structure. Perhaps the crest acted as a mast or a spar, and supported a brightly-coloured flap of skin. Perhaps different sizes of crest between individuals in the same herd helped the herd to recognize which of them was the leader.

Saurolophus, *one of the solid-crested duckbills*

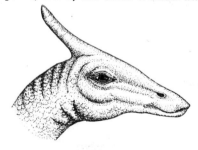

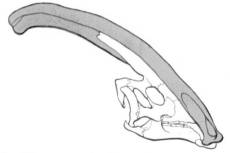

Skull of Parasaurolophus *showing the nasal bones*

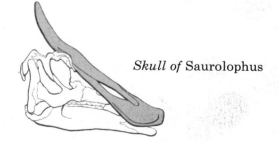

Skull of Saurolophus

Anatosaurus, *a broad-snouted flat-headed duckbill*

How did flat-headed duckbills live?

The flat-headed duckbills were more primitive than their crested cousins, but they were just as widespread and successful. A flat-headed duckbill, *Hadrosaurus* was the first dinosaur to be discovered in North America, in the 1850s. It was also the first skeleton to show that many of the dinosaurs walked on their hind legs.

The flat-headed duckbills and the crested types may not have come into contact with one another very often. They probably lived in different places. The crested forms would have lived in the open – where their crests and displays could be easily seen. The flat-headed types probably spent most of their time in thick woodland.

We know what dinosaur skin looked like from the remains of flat-headed duckbills. Many skeletons have been found with fossilized skin still covering them. The animals must have died and the bodies dried up before being buried.

The skin is very reptilian to look at. It consists of masses of closely-packed scales and is very wrinkled.

The flat-headed duckbills may have had voices as loud as those of their hollow-crested relatives. Many palaeontologists believe that the broad snout supported a flap of skin on the top of the head – a flap of skin that could be inflated with a croaking noise. Frogs can be seen doing this, by inflating pouches of skin at their throats. An evening woodland chorus of croaking duckbills must have made an awesome sound!

Fossilized skin of Anatosaurus

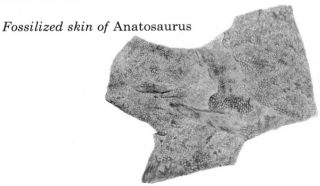

What other flat-headed duckbills were there?

Many of the flat-headed duckbills were very broad at the snout, like *Anatosaurus*, but in some the snouts were fairly narrow and the nose bones had evolved into a sturdy plate. *Brachylophosaurus* was a typical example.

This face-plate may have been used in combat – a bit like the bony head of the pachycephalosaurs (see page 88). When a young male challenged the leader of the herd, the two may have put their faces together and butted and pushed until one gave way. The face-plate would not have been much use as a serious weapon – it would not have been able to inflict much damage on a real enemy. When a big meat-eater approached, *Brachylophosaurus* or any other duckbill must have fled.

The duckbills were mostly fairly large animals. Seven to 10 metres (23 to 33 feet) was

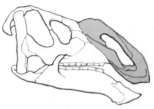

Skull of Brachylophosaurus, *showing the nasal bones forming the face-shield*

the average length. There were also small forms such as *Secernosaurus* and *Claosaurus*, both of which reached an adult length of between 3 and 4 metres (10 to 13 feet). The largest that we know is *Shantungosaurus* from China, reaching a length of about 15 metres (49 feet) and towering 7 metres (23 feet) above the ground. *Anatosaurus*, a fairly primitive flat-headed duckbill, was one of the last of the dinosaurs, surviving to the very end of the Cretaceous.

Brachylophosaurus, *a shield-faced flat-headed duckbill*

What is a ceratopsian?

Imagine a dinosaur like a rhinoceros – heavy body with strong legs, and horns on the face – that is a ceratopsian.

The ceratopsians were one of the last of the dinosaur groups to develop. They did not appear until the Upper Cretaceous and they lasted to the very end.

Their ancestors seem to have come from central Asia and migrated to North America. There they expanded into one of the most abundant and varied of the dinosaur groups. All the big ceratopsians lived in North America and their skeletons lie in the very last rocks of the Cretaceous period. There seem to have been no ceratopsians in South America, Africa, India or Australia. These continents had drifted away by the time they had developed.

How did the ceratopsians develop?

The earliest ceratopsians were quite small and not rhinoceros-like at all. However, they rapidly expanded.

The most distinctive thing about a ceratopsian was the head. It was covered by a heavy shield which expanded into a broad frill around the neck. The skull usually had horns as well. These pointed forward or upward, and must have made formidable weapons.

Early in their development the ceratopsians split into two main evolutionary lines. The first had very large frills and quite short horns. The second had much shorter frills and the horns grew into spectacular and dangerous structures.

(Opposite) Triceratops, *one of the best-known of the ceratopsians*

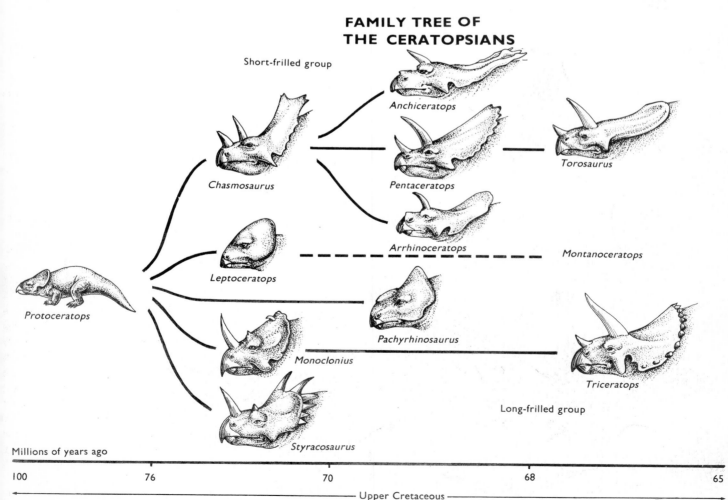

FAMILY TREE OF THE CERATOPSIANS

Short-frilled group

Anchiceratops

Chasmosaurus

Pentaceratops

Torosaurus

Arrhinoceratops

Leptoceratops

Montanoceratops

Protoceratops

Pachyrhinosaurus

Monoclonius

Triceratops

Styracosaurus

Long-frilled group

Millions of years ago

| 100 | 76 | 70 | 68 | 65 |

Upper Cretaceous

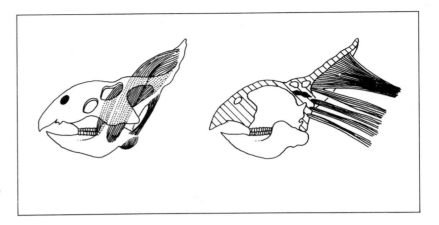

Skull of a primitive ceratopsian Protoceratops *showing the attachment of the jaw muscles* (left) *and the neck muscles* (right). *The neck frill probably first developed as an anchor point for the muscles*

What was the origin of the ceratopsians?

We must look for the ceratopsians' ancestors amongst the ornithopods of the Lower Cretaceous. We have seen how some ornithopods, such as *Camptosaurus* (page 86) were able to move on four legs as well as two. We have also seen how the front of an ornithopod's skull formed a kind of beak. In the ceratopsians this beak became more pronounced. Not only was there an extra toothless bone at the front of the lower jaw (the predentary) but there was also an extra one at the front of the upper jaw (the rostral bone). These bones would have been covered with a horny sheath, giving a powerful, hooked, eagle-like beak.

Finally we have seen an ornithopod that showed all these features and also had a heavy ridge that went round the back of the skull. It is not difficult to see that such a ridge could easily develop into the frill of a ceratopsian. This ornithopod was the parrot dinosaur, *Psittacosaurus* (see page 89).

How did the frill develop?

The bony frill of the ceratopsian was probably used to protect the neck, but it is likely that the frill started off as something else. The ceratopsian's beak was used for snipping off the plants that it ate. Its teeth were the chopping type rather than the grinding type so the jaws would have had to be very powerful. The strong jaw muscles would have needed to be attached to quite a large area. This area was probably provided by the ridge at the back of *Psittacosaurus'* skull. As the beak became more powerful and the jaws became stronger, the ridge would have become bigger to hold the muscles. It would have developed into the solid frill.

As the head grew bigger and heavier with all the bone and muscle, the neck muscles must have become stronger to hold it. These increased muscles would have needed a firm anchor. The back of the bony neck frill would have provided just such an anchor point and the heavy head would have been firmly fixed to the backbone. Later, when the heavy horns developed, there would have been enough muscle power in the neck to support them as well.

Amongst the more advanced ceratopsians the frill became more than a mere anchor-point for the muscles (see page 105). In some ceratopsians it was no longer the original solid plate of bone. Sometimes there were great holes through it – holes that were probably covered over by skin when the animal was alive. In more advanced forms these holes were filled with yet more bone.

Psittacosaurus (left), *some palaeontologists regard this as a specialized ornithopod, others as the most primitive of the ceratopsians*

98

Which was the most primitive ceratopsian?

The ancestral ceratopsian must have looked very much like *Leptoceratops*. It was about 1.8 metres (6 feet) long and lived in the Upper Cretaceous of North America. However, *Leptoceratops* existed quite late in the Cretaceous and most of the other ceratopsians had evolved by this time so it could not have been their ancestor. The most primitive ceratopsian must have been a late survivor of a primitive group.

There were five fingers on the hand, four toes on the foot, and the animal walked either on two feet or on all fours. Its frill was small but well-developed, but there was no sign of any horn. It must have looked like a frilled *Psittacosaurus*.

Leptoceratops, *a primitive ceratopsian*

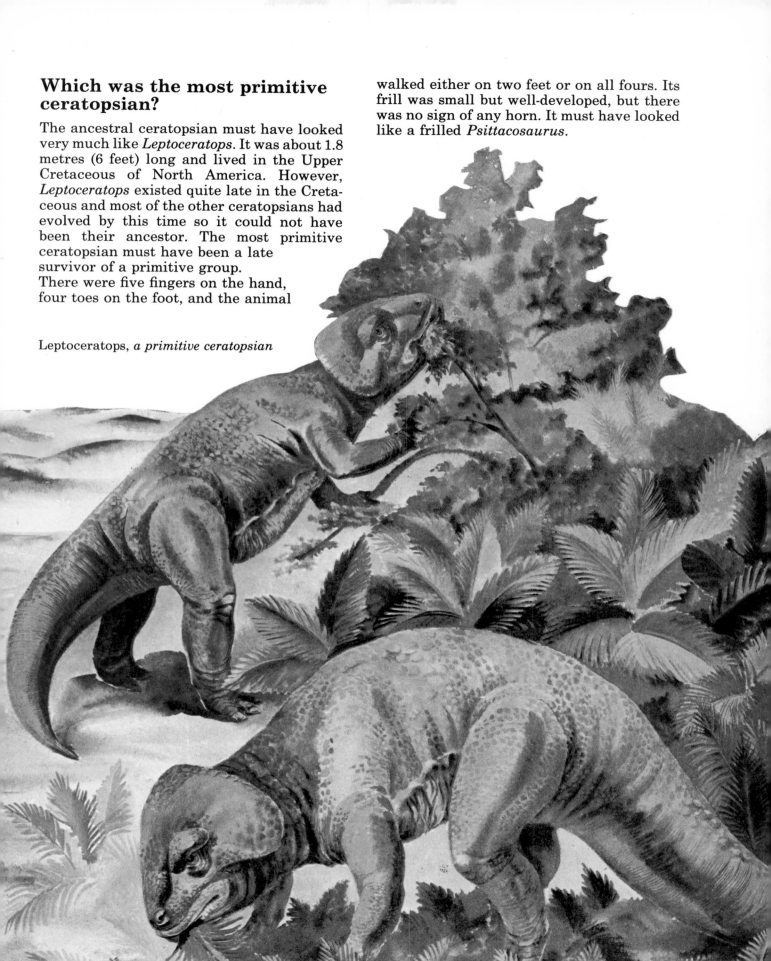

Protoceratops, *one of the earliest of the*
ceratopsians

Which was the smallest ceratopsian?

In the lowermost rocks of the Upper Cretaceous of China and Mongolia, there are the remains of a tiny, lightweight running dinosaur, just like *Hypsilophodon* (see page 85). However, there is a small frill at the back of its skull, showing it to be a ceratopsian, rather than an ornithopod. This animal is called *Microceratops gobiensis*, meaning 'little ceratopsian from the Gobi Desert', although there would have been no Gobi Desert there at the time that it lived. Instead, there would have been an area of lush vegetation that would have supported many plant-eating dinosaurs.

Which was the earliest ceratopsian?

The earliest true ceratopsian that we know is *Protoceratops* from the lower part of the Upper Cretaceous of Mongolia. It was about 2 metres (6.5 feet) long, had quite a heavy body and walked on all fours. The neck shield was quite large and swept back over the shoulders. It had no horns but a bump on the snout showed where horns would later evolve. The premaxilla bone that formed the upper part of the beak had two pairs of small teeth. Later ceratopsians lacked these.

Why is this animal famous?

Protoceratops gained worldwide stardom when its fossils were discovered in 1924 in the Gobi Desert of Mongolia by an expedition from the American Museum of Natural His-

Fossilized Protoceratops *eggs*

tory. The remains of more than a hundred animals were discovered, at all stages of growth. What is more important, their nests and eggs were found there as well. It was the first time that anyone had any proof that the dinosaurs laid eggs. The nests had been hollows scooped in the sand, and in these the *Protoceratops* females had laid a dozen or so eggs in concentric circles, with the narrow ends pointing inwards. Some nests had considerably more eggs than this, suggesting that more than one female may have used the same hollow.

The animal's full scientific name is *Protoceratops andrewsi*, after the leader of this famous expedition, Roy Chapman Andrews.

Did *Protoceratops* have any enemies?

For all its success *Protoceratops* seems to have been beset by foes.

In 1971 a remarkable fossil was found by palaeontologists in Mongolia. It consisted of a *Protoceratops* skeleton tangled up with the skeleton of another dinosaur. The other dinosaur was *Velociraptor* – one of the sickle-clawed dinosaurs. It was about 1.8 metres (6 feet) long, with a long head and quite a small sickle claw.

Palaeontologists believe that this is the remains of a battle that took place about 100 million years ago. The *Velociraptor* may have attacked the *Protoceratops* and tried to kill it with its sickle-claw. It had grabbed hold of the head-shield and was in the act of ripping at its throat, when the *Protoceratops* brought up its beak and plunged it into its enemy's belly. What happened then we shall never know. The two seem to have died at that moment and were fossilized in that position.

At another locality a *Protoceratops* nest was discovered with the skeleton of a small ostrich-dinosaur in it. This stranger has been called *Oviraptor philoceratops* meaning 'the egg-stealer that was fond of ceratopsians'. It could be that the ostrich-dinosaur was in the act of robbing the nest when it was overwhelmed by a sandstorm!

Apart from such obvious signs of trouble, all dinosaurs would have been subject to the diseases and parasites that affect the rest of the animal world. However, usually these do not show up in the fossil record.

Monoclonius, *a 6 m (20 ft) short-frilled ceratopsian that roamed the flowering woodlands of Upper Cretaceous North America*

Where did the ceratopsians live?

The protoceratopsians and their immediate ancestors, the psittacosaurs, lived in central Asia. The larger and more advanced forms seem to have lived entirely in North America. It seems that after the group evolved, they crossed to the neighbouring continent via the land bridge that existed where the Bering Strait now lies, and flourished there. Remains of some of the later protoceratopsians lie in North American Upper Cretaceous rocks. We do not know for sure that there were no advanced ceratopsians in Asia – it may be that we have not found Asian rocks of the right age.

What did the advanced ceratopsians eat?

If we look at the teeth of any animal we can tell something about what it ate.

The cheek teeth of a ceratopsian were sharp and worked with a scissors action, and the beak at the front was quite strong. The huge cheek muscles attached to the frill made this arrangement very powerful.

It looks as though the ceratopsians developed so that they could feed on a new and tougher type of vegetation that evolved during the second half of the Cretaceous period.

The flowering plants developed at that time, and there were forests of the kinds of trees that we would recognize today. Palm trees, birches, magnolias, poplars, plane trees and willows grew in woodlands across the North American continent, along with the conifers and ferns that had been there for many millions of years. The ceratopsians would have browsed amongst these colourful forests for food.

How did they live?

Most plant-eating dinosaurs appear to have lived in herds. The big ceratopsians would have been no exception. Indeed their remains are so plentiful in some places that they must have been herd animals, roaming the groves and forests of the Upper Cretaceous uplands of North America.

They probably moved from place to place with the young at the centre of the herd. If danger threatened they may have formed a protective ring around them, presenting a fearsome barrier of horns and shields to an oncoming enemy. The large males may have then charged the attacker and driven it off.

What was a short-frilled ceratopsian?

The short-frilled line of the ceratopsians had a fairly small frill but an enormous nose horn.

Usually there was only a horn on the nose and none above the eyes but sometimes horns grew in both positions. *Monoclonius* was a typical short-frilled ceratopsian. It had a single nose horn over 70 centimetres (28 inches) long and only a pair of small bumps at the horn-sites over the eyes.

Were there hornless hornheads?

Although it sounds like nonsense, there were ceratopsians that had no horns. *Pachyrhinosaurus* was a typical short-frilled ceratopsian about 5.5 metres (18 feet) long. However, its frill was so short that it was almost non-existent, and there was no sign at all of horns on its face. Instead there was a heavy bony lump in front of and between the eyes. The obvious use of such a lump would have been as a battering ram, and could have been used to knock down the tree-ferns and cycads to reach the feathery leaves on which it fed. A bony lump would have been even more efficient at this than would have been the conventional set of horns. It could also have been used in contests to find the leader of the herd, just like the heavy skulls of the bone-heads (see page 88). Again this would have been more efficient than the horns of the typical ceratopsians. However, a bony lump would not have been much good as a weapon. If a meat-eater attacked there was neither horn nor shield area to fend it off. It could be that *Pachyrhinosaurus* lived in an area where there were no meat-eaters, which seems unlikely, or else it had some other form of defence that does not show up in the fossils. Its remains are found in the Upper Cretaceous rocks of Canada.

Were all the advanced ceratopsians big animals?

Most of the later ceratopsians were big fellows, usually upwards of about 5.5 metres (18 feet) long, but in the Upper Cretaceous of Montana there was one called *Brachyceratops* which reached a length of only 2.5 metres (8 feet). Apart from its light build it was very much like the other advanced ceratopsians, with a short but well-developed frill and a good long nose horn. However, some palaeontologists think that *Brachyceratops* was nothing more than a baby *Monoclonius*.

Styracosaurus *at full charge. This 6 m (20 ft) long short-frilled ceratopsian from the Upper Cretaceous of Alberta and Montana must have been a formidable adversary for any meat-eater of the time*

What was the frill's main purpose?

Look at this picture of a charging *Styracosaurus*! It must have been a terrifying sight! It is mostly the spikes on the frill that make the appearance so alarming. Many animals today puff themselves up, or rely on expanding frills, to make themselves look more fearsome to an enemy. A ceratopsian frill may have been used for the same kind of threat display.

What was a long-frilled ceratopsian?

Styracosaurus, for all its spikes, was as much a short-frilled ceratopsian as was *Monoclonius*. If we look at a side view of the head we can see that the frill is quite short and that the spikes are growing out of its margin. It also has the huge nose horn and the tiny eyebrow horns of the other short-frilled ceratopsians.

A long-frilled ceratopsian could give a similar threat display to an enemy by raising a solid shield that normally spread back over the neck and shoulders. *Chasmosaurus* was a typical long-frilled ceratopsian. It had a huge triangular shield which would have lifted to an impressive height when the animal lowered its head. As in all other long-frilled ceratopsians, *Chasmosaurus*'s eyebrow horns were quite well developed and its nose horn was quite small compared with those of *Monoclonius* and *Styracosaurus*.

The three horns of *Chasmosaurus* were typical of the group as a whole, but there were differences. *Arrhinoceratops* had hardly any nose horn at all, while *Pentaceratops* had three horns and a pair of spikes jutting out from the corner of the upper jaw giving it a five-horned appearance.

What was a ceratopsian body like?

The shape of the head differed from ceratopsian to ceratopsian. However, these widely varying heads were all mounted on very similarly-shaped bodies.

Although the protoceratopsian body was low and may have been somewhat sprawling, the advanced ceratopsians had heavy rhinoceros-like bodies. The great mass of flesh and bone was supported by strong pillar-like hind legs. Their front legs tended to stick out at the elbows, giving a broad base for the weight of the head.

Chasmosaurus, *a 5 m (16 ft) long example of the long-frilled ceratopsians. The bone of the shield had wide openings to keep the weight down*

How big were ceratopsians?

There was a *Microceratops* from the Upper Cretaceous of China that was the size of a rabbit. However, it was so primitive that some palaeontologists think that it was related to the hypsilophodonts.

Protoceratops was quite small for a dinosaur – only about 2 metres (6.5 feet) long. The later ceratopsians became progressively larger. The last of the line was the mighty *Triceratops*, one of the best-known and most popular of the dinosaurs. It had a length of up to 9 metres (29.5 feet), a third of which was head and frill. It stood about 2 metres (6.5 feet) high at the hip and must have weighed something like 5.5 tonnes. The bony cores of the eyebrow-horns were each about 90 centimetres (35 inches) long, and so these horns must have been huge.

How widespread was *Triceratops*?

Triceratops breaks the rules! We have seen that the short-frilled ceratopsians such as *Monoclonius* had a long nose-horn and short eyebrow-horns, and that the long-frilled types like *Chasmosaurus* had long eyebrow-horns and a short nose-horn. *Triceratops* was one of the short-crested line – but look at the eyebrow-horns it sported!

Triceratops was the last of the ceratopsians and its remains are found in Upper Cretaceous rocks of Wyoming, Colorado, Montana, Alberta and Saskatchewan. Palaeontologists recognize at least 15 different species of the creature, each one differing in the shape of the head and horns. The largest species was *Triceratops horridus* and this is the one that usually appears in books. Others had narrower frills, shorter eyebrow-horns or even longer nose-horns.

Triceratops, *the largest of the ceratopsians*

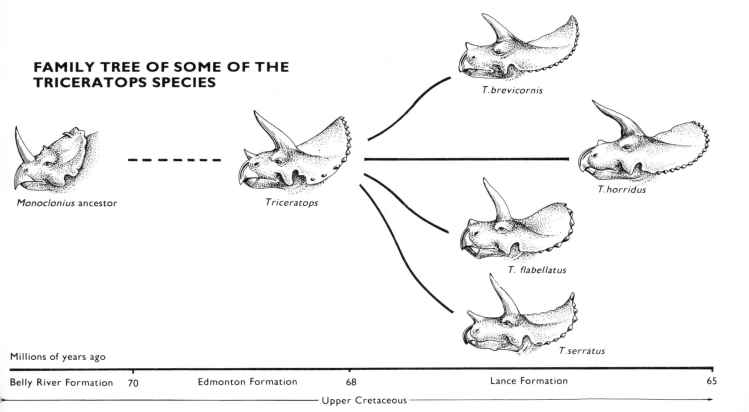

FAMILY TREE OF SOME OF THE TRICERATOPS SPECIES

Monoclonius ancestor

Triceratops

T.brevicornis

T.horridus

T. flabellatus

T.serratus

Millions of years ago

| Belly River Formation | 70 | Edmonton Formation | 68 | Lance Formation | 65 |

Upper Cretaceous

How do we know there were so many species?

Usually when a dinosaur skeleton is fossilized the first thing that breaks up and is lost is the skull. Most dinosaurs had very light skulls – mere frameworks of bony struts. How different was the skull of *Triceratops*! It was a mass of solid bone from beak to frill and would remain long after the rest of the skeleton was lost.

How did *Triceratops* live?

We can imagine *Triceratops* following the same lifestyle as the other big ceratopsians (see page 103). They must have moved in herds across the uplands of the North American landscape, browsing in the glades and woodlands within sight of the young Rocky Mountains. It was a time of changing climate and changing vegetation. Since *Triceratops* survived for several million years after the other big ceratopsians, it must have been able to eat some of the new vegetation that would not support the rest.

The herds probably had quite a strict social structure, with a big bull *Triceratops* to lead the herd. This would have consisted of several females, some young males and the babies. Once in a while one of the young bulls would challenge the leader to gain control of the herd and the females. They would then fight, but not to the death. They would probably have locked horns and pushed and shoved – each one trying to win by its superior strength. Eventually one of them would tire and back off, leaving the other in control.

Triceratops *skull, a solid lump of bone*

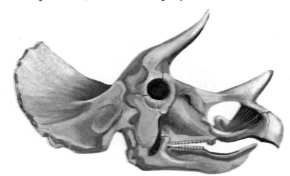

107

Any flesh-eating dinosaur of the time would have had difficulty in fighting *Triceratops*. If attacked it would have just stood its ground and faced its enemy. The pillar-like back legs would have borne the weight of the body, while its widely-spaced forelimbs could have turned the body round to keep its horns and shield pointed towards the danger. Any meat-eater would have had to be content with a youngster that had become separated from the herd, or an old and dying bull that the herd had discarded.

During a fight a *Triceratops'* body would have been as sturdy as a blockhouse. The narrow base of the hind legs and the broad base of the forelegs would have made it very difficult to move the great body, whether by its own kind or a meat-eater.

We know that *Triceratops* fought one another and possibly other creatures. Palaeontologists have found their skulls with deep injuries on the shields. Some have even had horns broken off and survived the damage, the stumps healing very well.

When was it discovered?

Bits of *Triceratops* were discovered in 1887, but at that time nobody knew what they were. They consisted of nothing more than a pair of horn points. The finder took them to the famous palaeontologist, Othniel Charles Marsh (see page 153), who thought that they belonged to some kind of buffalo. He gave it the scientific name *Bison alticornis*. Two years later a complete skull was found and the name *Triceratops horridus* was given to it.

A meat-eater such as Tyrannosaurus *would have had great difficulty breaking through the defences of a healthy and active* Triceratops

109

Kentrosaurus, *a spiny stegosaur from the Upper Jurassic of east Africa*

What is a stegosaur?

The stegosaurs were the slow-moving armoured dinosaurs of the Jurassic period. Their armour consisted of a series of broad plates and narrow spines along the back and tail. They evolved in the Lower Jurassic, from primitive bird-hipped dinosaurs such as *Scelidosaurus*. Palaeontologists once thought that *Scelidosaurus* was the first stegosaur, but now they think it belonged to the next armoured group – the ankylosaurs (see page 117).

Most of the stegosaur remains consist of isolated plates and spines, with no skeleton to stick them on, so it is very difficult to work out how many stegosaurs there were, what they looked like and how they evolved. However, there do seem to have been two main evolutionary lines. The first had an armour that consisted mostly of plates. The other were protected mostly by spines.

The earliest true stegosaurs date from the Middle Jurassic and lived in Europe and Asia. They reached their peak in the Upper Jurassic when they lived in North America, China and Africa. A few existed into Cretaceous times and there was even one found in the Upper Cretaceous of India.

Scelidosaurus, *a primitive ankylosaur that was close to the ancestral stock of the stegosaurs*

SUGGESTED FAMILY TREE OF THE STEGOSAURS

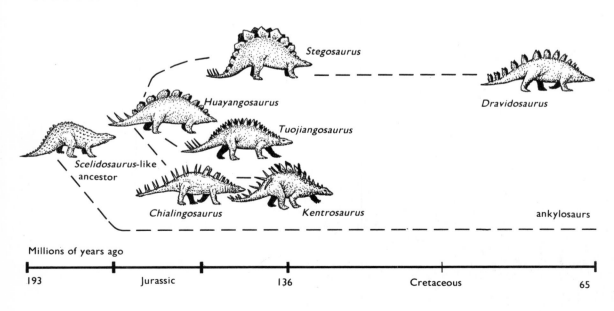

Stegosaurus

Huayangosaurus

Tuojiangosaurus

Dravidosaurus

Scelidosaurus-like ancestor

Chialingosaurus

Kentrosaurus

ankylosaurs

Millions of years ago

193   Jurassic   136   Cretaceous   65

Stegosaurus, *the best known of the stegosaurs*

Which was the best-known stegosaur?

The best known stegosaur must be *Stegosaurus* itself – the creature that gave its name to the whole group. Indeed it is just about the only stegosaur that is known in any detail. It was certainly the largest, growing to a length of about 9 metres (30 feet) and standing about twice the height of a man at the hips.

The armour consisted of a double row of flat plates that ran down its back from just behind its head to half way down its tail. There were about a dozen pairs of these, the largest being above the hips, and they were triangular in shape. At the end of the tail were two pairs of long spines, probably used as weapons.

The skull was long and narrow. The teeth were weak and *Stegosaurus* had a toothless predentary bone at the front of the lower jaw – just as in all bird-hipped dinosaurs.

How did it live?

Stegosaurus remains have been found in the Morrison Formation of North America. It lived in the forested swamps and backwaters of this river plain during the Upper Jurassic, sharing its habitat with the big sauropods such as *Apatosaurus* (see page 71), and the theropods like *Allosaurus* and *Ceratosaurus* (see page 56).

Like all other bird-hipped dinosaurs, *Stegosaurus* ate plants. With its weak teeth it could hardly have eaten anything else. The forelimbs were shorter than the hind, so the head was held quite near the ground. It probably fed on the low-growing vegetation such as ferns and horsetails. Since most of the weight was concentrated around the hips, *Stegosaurus* may have been able to rear up on its hind legs for brief periods to reach low-hanging fronds and leaves. We don't know if it lived in herds, in pairs or singly.

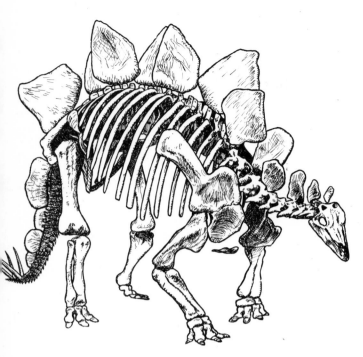

Stegosaurus *skeleton*

How were the plates arranged?

It is difficult to tell exactly how the plates of *Stegosaurus* were arranged on the animal. As they were not fixed to the skeleton palaeontologists usually find them as a scattered jumble. On most restorations they are shown sticking up in pairs. This would give them the same arrangement as the spines on the other stegosaurs. Sometimes they are shown staggered. This would be sensible if the plates were used for warming and cooling the body. One or two people have suggested that they lay flat. That way they would make a better armour. We just do not know what *Stegosaurus* looked like.

Three restorations of Stegosaurus *showing its plates arranged vertically in pairs, vertically staggered and horizontally*

What were the plates for?

This is a question that has been vexing palaeontologists for a long, long time. The traditional view is that the plates of *Stegosaurus* were used for protection. If the animal was attacked by a large theropod, such as *Allosaurus* that towered above it, the vulnerable backbone would have been protected against the teeth. *Stegosaurus* could then have swung its spiked tail from side to side and injured its attacker. The trouble with this theory is that the plates were not fixed into the skeleton as they should have been to make an efficient armour. They were merely embedded in the skin.

The second theory was that the plates acted as radiators, helping to keep the *Stegosaurus* at an even temperature. They would have had the same function as the sails of *Dimetrodon* (see page 35) or *Spinosaurus* (see page 59). However, if that had been the case, why did other stegosaurs such as *Kentrosaurus* have spines instead of plates? Spines would have been no good as heat-exchangers.

A third possibility is that they were a display or a threat device, like the towering neck shield of the long-frilled ceratopsians (see page 105).

Tuojiangosaurus, *an Upper Jurassic Chinese stegosaur*

Where are stegosaur remains found?

As we have seen, the stegosaurs lived mostly in Europe, Asia, North America and east Africa. Their remains lie in Middle and Upper Jurassic rocks of these areas. Almost the whole group seems to have died out early in the Cretaceous period. They were replaced by another group of armoured dinosaurs – the ankylosaurs.

The exception to this is *Dravidosaurus* – a stegosaur from the Upper Cretaceous of India. The reason for this may be the changing geography of the times. India broke away from the main landmass and became an island in the Cretaceous. It may have acted as a kind of 'lost world' on which the stegosaurs survived without interference from ankylosaurs. A bone that might have come from an ankylosaur has been found in the Cretaceous rocks of India, but many palaeontologists believe that it actually came from another stegosaur.

Both spiny and plated forms of stegosaur lived in China. Unfortunately most of the remains are just odd pieces and we cannot tell what the animal looked like. *Chialingosaurus* is one such. The restoration shown here is made from very fragmentary pieces. We don't know how accurate it is. It may be that the pieces belonged to another specimen of the neighbouring *Tuojiangosaurus*, or even to the African spined form, *Kentrosaurus*.

Chialingosaurus, *a Middle Jurassic Chinese stegosaur*

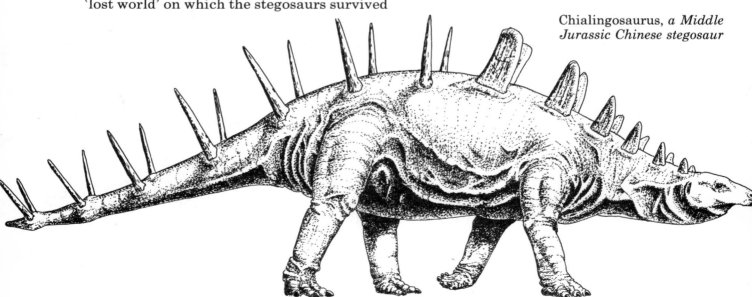

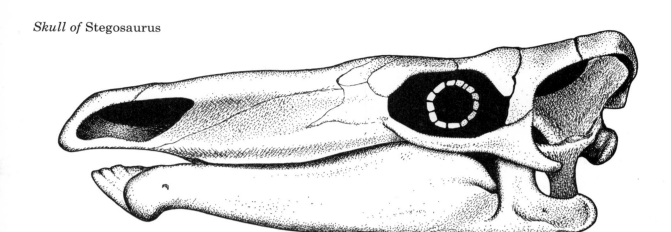

Did stegosaurs really have two brains?

Look at this illustration of the skull of a *Stegosaurus*. It is very small and narrow compared with the rest of the body. There was no room for much brain inside there. This has led some palaeontologists to suspect that much of the control of the body – especially around the hind legs and tail – was carried out by an extra nerve centre situated in the hips. This would not have been a second brain – just a sort of an amplifier to boost the signal from

the brain itself. This gave rise to the popular notion that *Stegosaurus* had two brains. Similar theories have been put forward about the sauropods (see page 67). In fact, there was a large space in the hip, where the spinal cord passed through. This would have held something that would have been many times larger than the animal's brain.

Not all palaeontologists agree with this interpretation. Some say that the cavity contained a gland that produced glycogen – an animal starch that provided an energy supply. Modern birds have such a gland.

Skeleton of Stegosaurus, *showing the possible position of the extra nerve centre in the hips*

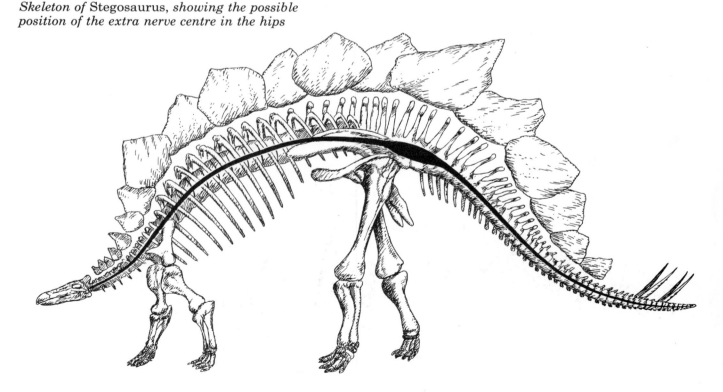

What is an ankylosaur?

The last group of dinosaurs that we shall consider consists of the heavily armoured types – the reptilian tanks. These were the ankylosaurs.

Unlike the stegosaurs, their armour was not merely embedded in the skin. The armour of an ankylosaur was firmly fused to the skeleton. Unlike the ceratopsians, the weapons were not built into the head. The weapons of an ankylosaur, if it had any at all, were mounted on the tail.

The ankylosaurs were bird-hipped dinosaurs and, like all other bird-hipped dinosaurs, they ate plants. However, the characteristic bird shape of the hip is difficult to see. The great weight and compact nature of the armour meant that nearly all the bony structures beneath had to be modified to carry the huge mass. The hip became a solid lump of bone with all the separate bones fused together and the gaps filled. The ankylosaurs ranged in size from less than 2 metres (6.5 feet) long, up to about 10 metres (33 feet). The largest would have weighed several tonnes.

We know of many different kinds of ankylosaur – over 30 in fact. However, as usual, most of them are only known from a few isolated scraps of bone.

When did the ankylosaurs live?

Palaeontologists think that the armour of an ankylosaur was a very primitive feature. In other words, it was very much like the armour of the dinosaurs' ancient ancestors. In this respect the group does not seem to have evolved much from the very early days. However, nearly all ankylosaur remains come from Upper Cretaceous rocks – the very end of the age of dinosaurs.

The earliest ankylosaur is the Lower Jurassic *Scelidosaurus* from southern England. This is, indeed, the earliest Jurassic dinosaur that we know about. There must have been other ankylosaurs living throughout Jurassic times before they evolved into the Cretaceous forms that we know. During this time they developed into two evolutionary lines. One line consisted of fairly light beasts with narrow heads and no tail weapons. The other line consisted of the great squat tanks, bristling with armour and a wicked club or set of spikes on the tail. The lightly-built types lived mostly in Europe and North America, while the heavy forms were mostly Asian, with a few North American species.

Ankylosaurs are very rare as fossils. This is why we do not know much about their early history. They probably lived in uplands where no sediments were formed.

(Opposite) Scelidosaurus, *the earliest ankylosaur*

What other group could this animal have belonged to? (See page 111)

FAMILY TREE OF THE ANKYLOSAURS

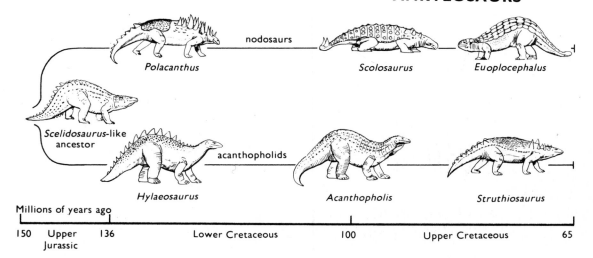

nodosaurs

Polacanthus   *Scolosaurus*   *Euoplocephalus*

Scelidosaurus-like ancestor

acanthopholids

Hylaeosaurus   *Acanthopholis*   *Struthiosaurus*

Millions of years ago

| 150 | Upper Jurassic | 136 | Lower Cretaceous | 100 | Upper Cretaceous | 65 |

117

The armour of a heavy ankylosaur, such as Ankylosaurus, *was a tightly-packed mosaic of bony plates across the back*

What was primitive ankylosaur armour like?

The armour of an ankylosaur consisted of bony plates, called scutes. Many of the ancestral thecodonts had these bony plates embedded in their skin. However, most dinosaurs lost them as they evolved. Some other dinosaurs still kept them, such as *Hypsilophodon* (see page 85), but the ankylosaurs were the only group in which they developed to any great extent.

In the primitive ankylosaurs, like *Scelidosaurus*, and the lightly-built types such as *Acanthopholis*, the armour consisted of rows of scutes, all separated from one another. Sometimes these scutes had a ridge along them. Sometimes the ridge was extended into a vertical plate, like that of a stegosaur. Sometimes they developed into long spines. When that happened the spines grew along the flanks, but sometimes they were on the tail or on the neck.

What was advanced ankylosaur armour like?

In the advanced ankylosaurs, such as *Ankylosaurus* itself, the armour was very heavy, compact and sturdy. The plates sometimes developed into a tight mosaic, often with small plates fixed over the ribs and larger ones in rows between. In some ankylosaurs there was a solid shield over the hips. The armour was often fused to the hip bones and the hip girdle degenerated into an unrecognizable mass of bone. Sometimes the neck became so plated with armour that it was too stiff to turn.

The head was short and broad. The armour plates on the head were fused to the skull, turning the skull into a continuous bony lump. This was not at all like the open framework with gaps and hollows that most other dinosaurs possessed for a skull.

Ankylosaur skeletons are usually found upside down. A dead one in the water would turn over because of the armour's weight.

What was the ankylosaur skull like?

The head of the more primitive ankylosaurs was quite long and narrow. That of the more advanced forms was short and broad. Both had the toothless beak at the front, shared by the rest of the bird-hipped dinosaurs.

We have seen that the skull of the advanced forms was so plated with armour that it had become encased in a continuous shell of bone. Inside it the structure was supported by a framework of struts that gave it a honeycomb structure. The nasal passages were long winding tunnels in this structure and may have helped to warm the air on the way to the lungs.

By far the most important thing about the skull is the fact that there was a shelf of bone – a palate – that separated the nasal passages from the mouth. Mammals have this, and it means that the animal can eat and breathe at the same time. This made it the most advanced of the dinosaur skulls.

How primitive were Cretaceous ankylosaurs?

After a long period from the emergence of *Scelidosaurus* in the Lower Jurassic, the lightly-built ankylosaurs reappeared in the lower part of the Late Cretaceous with *Acanthopholis*. They obviously had not changed much in the intervening 30 million years. *Acanthopholis* looked very much like its Jurassic ancestor. It had a robust body, with stout legs, a fairly long tail and a long neck. The armour consisted of several rows of rectangular bony plates embedded in the skin, running fore and aft. There were also two rows of triangular spikes along the neck. The animal had a length of about 5 metres (16 feet).

Acanthopholis, *a primitive, lightly-built ankylosaur from the Cretaceous of southern England*

119

Polacanthus, *an early heavy ankylosaur from the Lower Cretaceous of southern England What other animals lived here at the same time?* (See pages 40–41)

Which was the earliest heavy ankylosaur?

Polacanthus, from the Lower Cretaceous of southern England, is the earliest heavy ankylosaur that we know about. Even so it was quite lightly-built and resembled *Acantholis* in overall appearance. In fact, some palaeontologists regard *Polacanthus* as one of the lightly-built line. It was about 4 metres (13 feet) long, and lived amongst the shoreline beds of horsetails that grew along the edge of the vast inland Wealden lake that stretched from southern England to Belgium at that time. The skull has never been found but we think that it must have looked just like other ankylosaur skulls.

What was *Polacanthus* armour like?

The armour, as well as the general build, of *Polacanthus* was similar to that of one of the lightly-built ankylosaurs. It had a double row of enormous spines, 14 in all, along the neck and shoulders. A double row of vertical plates stretched down to the end of the tail. The rest of the armour was in the form of small oval plates embedded in the skin. However, the main armour feature, and the one that makes it one of the heavier ankylosaurs, was a solid flat shield that covered the hips. This was rectangular in shape and made up of a fused mass of bony scutes.

The reason that some palaeontologists regard *Polacanthus* as one of the more primitive of the ankylosaurs is that none of this armour was fused to the skeleton. It was just embedded in the skin. Also like other lightly-built ankylosaurs, *Polacanthus* lived in Europe. The later, heavy forms seem to have been confined to Asia and North America.

A famous skeleton of *Polacanthus* is mounted in the British Museum (Natural History) in London. It is complete except for the skull and the feet.

How did the heavy ankylosaurs stand?

The heavy ankylosaurs, such as *Scolosaurus*, had such a weight of armour on their back that the body became broad and squat to carry it. At the same time the legs became very stout.

Sprawing stance of an early reptile

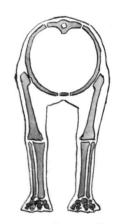

Upright stance of most dinosaurs

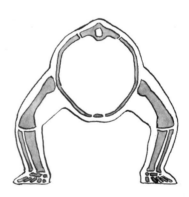

Sprawling stance of the heavy ankylosaurs

They were heavy and strong, and became splayed outwards. All other dinosaurs had an upright stance, with the legs held directly under the body. Ankylosaurs reverted to a more old-fashioned way of walking, in a sprawling posture with the legs out at the sides. The sophisticated structure of the hip bones (see page 42) that developed with the upright stance in other dinosaurs, was lost in the ankylosaurs, and the hips were just a fused mass of bone.

Scolosaurus had a weapon on its tail consisting of a pair of spikes

What weapons did ankylosaurs have?

The lightly-built ankylosaurs had no weapons to speak of – just their various forms of armour. The heavily-built forms, on the other hand, had even more armour and they had weapons as well.

The skeleton of *Scolosaurus* shows two bumps on the end of the tail. These bumps must have held a pair of great spikes.

Ankylosaurs, such as Euoplocephalus, *with a club on the tail would have been able to defend themselves against the big meat-eaters of the day*

The more common type of weapon is that found on *Ankylosaurus*. This consisted of a kind of club made of two lobes of bone. The vertebrae of the tail were lashed together by tendons that had turned into bone, making the tail a good stiff shaft for the club. These weapons could have been swung against an enemy, such as an attacking carnosaur, with the full weight of the armoured tail behind them.

Ankylosaurus, *the largest and the last of the ankylosaurs, would have had nothing to fear from the great carnosaurs*

Which was the largest ankylosaur?

The largest ankylosaur that we know about is also the last to have existed. It is, indeed, the only ankylosaur that we have found dating from the very end of the Cretaceous. It is *Ankylosaurus* itself.

It was over 10 metres (33 feet) long and its head was the usual compact shell of bone. It had a broad toothless beak at the front and at the back four spines stuck out, looking rather like ears. The armour was a mass of rectangular plates and there was the usual club at the end of the tail.

Which was the smallest ankylosaur?

Again we can only mention the smallest that we know about. This was *Struthiosaurus* which was only about 1.8 metres (6 feet) long. It had an armour of spines over the neck and plates over the body and tail. One of the lightly-built ankylosaurs, it lived in southern Europe in the Upper Cretaceous. It was also one of the last to have existed.

Some palaeontologists think that it was small because it lived on islands. We tend to find dwarf animals living on islands even today.

Palaeoscincus, *the earliest anklyosaur to be found*

Which was the first ankylosaur to be discovered?

Some fossil teeth were found in 1855 in Montana. These proved to be the first dinosaur remains to be discovered in North America. They were picked up by a Dr Ferdinand Vandiveer Hayden and taken to the famous palaeontologist Joseph Leidy. Leidy thought that they came from a lizard and gave it the name *Palaeoscincus* meaning 'ancient skink'. Later remains showed that the teeth belonged to an ankylosaur.

Palaeoscincus was one of the heavily-built ankylosaurs, about 5 metres (16 feet) long. Its armour consisted of rows of rectangular plates that ran across the back from side to side. Its armour also had long heavy spines sticking out at the sides, rather like a Japanese roof.

Since then, as usual in palaeontology, other researchers have found that this animal might be the same as another animal that was discovered about the same time and given the name *Edmontonia*. Some palaeontologists think that *Edmontonia* should be the proper scientific name for *Palaeoscincus*.

There is the same kind of confusion about the name *Ankylosaurus*. *Ankylosaurus*, the animal after which the whole group was named, was first discovered in Canada in 1902. The palaeontologist gave it the scientific name *Stereocephalus*. What happened then was something that often happens in palaeontology. The palaeontologist found that the name had already been given to another animal so he replaced it with the name *Euoplocephalus*. Meanwhile somebody else had found more remains of the same animal and called it *Ankylosaurus*. Now we

think that the two sets of remains belong to different animals, so there was both a *Euoplocephalus* and an *Ankylosaurus*.

Palaeontology is full of muddles like this, which is why you will find some books saying one thing and some another. It is not that one is wrong and the other right. It is just that we are learning all the time and nobody can be really sure of what happened in the distant past.

How did the ankylosaurs live?

The ankylosaurs became the important armoured dinosaurs as soon as the stegosaurs died out. This suggests that the two groups lived in a similar environment and ate the same sort of food. That is what happens when one group of animals becomes extinct – another evolves to take its place.

However, heavily-armoured dinosaurs would not have enjoyed living in the swampy forests that supported the stegosaurs. It is much more likely that they were upland animals.

Most of the ankylosaur skeletons have been discovered lying upside down in river sediments. It looks as if they died in the mountains and were washed down to the lowlands. The weight of the armour turned them on their backs as they were swirled along in the current. When they sank to the bottom they were buried and fossilized in that position. Ankylosaur fossils have even been found in marine deposits, showing they had been washed all the way out to sea.

(Opposite) Scolosaurus

Why did it have spikes on it tail? (See page 122)

What creatures flew during the Mesozoic?

We have seen that wherever there is a place in which some creature may live, something will evolve to live in it. The air is no exception. As soon as insects evolved during the Devonian period, they took to flying. They have been flying ever since.

For insects flying is easy. They are very light and can be easily blown about by the wind. Flying is more difficult for a bigger animal – it has to lift its weight off the ground. The amphibians did not evolve any flying forms in the early days as far as we know. However, once the reptiles had evolved, some of them experimented with flight.

One of the first was *Kuehneosaurus*, a kind of a Triassic lizard, 75 centimetres (29.5 inches) long that lived in central England. It had long spines that grew sideways from its ribs, supporting a pair of web-like wings. In this it resembled the tiny 'flying dragon' lizard of modern Malaysia. It must have been able to glide from the rocky desert cliffs in which it lived. The same kind of wing evolved in another lizard, *Icarosaurus*, which lived in the eastern United States at that time.

How did flight develop?

There is a difference between gliding and flying. An animal that glides just stretches its wings and floats on the air without much effort. An animal that flies must flap its wings to get off the ground and stay in the air. It is quite certain that gliding creatures evolved first, and from them the flying creatures developed.

Nowadays the true flying creatures are the birds. These are the most important group of vertebrate animals in the skies, although the flying mammals – the bats – are also very successful.

Back in the age of dinosaurs the most important flying animals were a group of flying reptiles called the pterosaurs.

How did pterosaurs evolve?

The pterosaurs evolved firstly as gliding reptiles. Their Triassic ancestor, *Podopteryx*, looked like a lizard but had a broad flap of skin that stretched from the body and tail along the long hind legs. It could glide with this. By the Jurassic these flaps of skin had evolved into proper wings and the forelimbs had become adapted for flight.

Opposite *Flying insects abounded during the age of dinosaurs*

Kuehneosaurus, *a gliding reptile from the Triassic*

Rhamphorhynchus, *a primitive pterosaur*

What does 'pterosaur' mean?

The word means 'winged lizard'. The wing of a pterosaur was supported by a very long and strong fourth finger. The first three fingers were left as a little hand half way along the front edge. The bones of this long finger were as thick as those of the arm. The trailing edge of the wing was attached to the legs and tail. The wing was a simple expanse of skin, like a bat has between its fingers.

The wings of a pterosaur, a bird and a bat compared

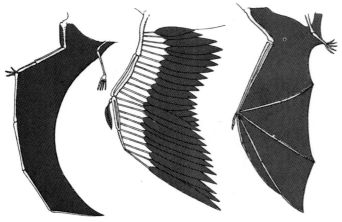

What was a primitive pterosaur like?

The most primitive pterosaurs had long thin wings and long tails. *Rhamphorhynchus* from the Upper Jurassic of Germany and East Africa, was a typical member of this group.

Rhamphorhynchus' skeleton has been found in shallow-water lagoon and river sediments. It probably lived on fish that it snatched from the water as it swooped low. It had the right type of teeth for this. It was quite a small beast – about the size of a crow.

It had quite a flexible neck, allowing the head to be held bird-like at right angles to it. The tail was long and stiff, with the backbones lashed together with strong tendons. At the end of the tail there was a diamond-shaped flap of skin, so the tail may have been used as a kind of a rudder.

We know about the skin of the wings and the flap on the end of the tail because of the way the animal was fossilized. In southern Germany it was embedded in a very fine limestone that preserved the impression of these soft parts. It was the same limestone that preserved the shapes of the feathers of *Archaeopteryx* (see page 50).

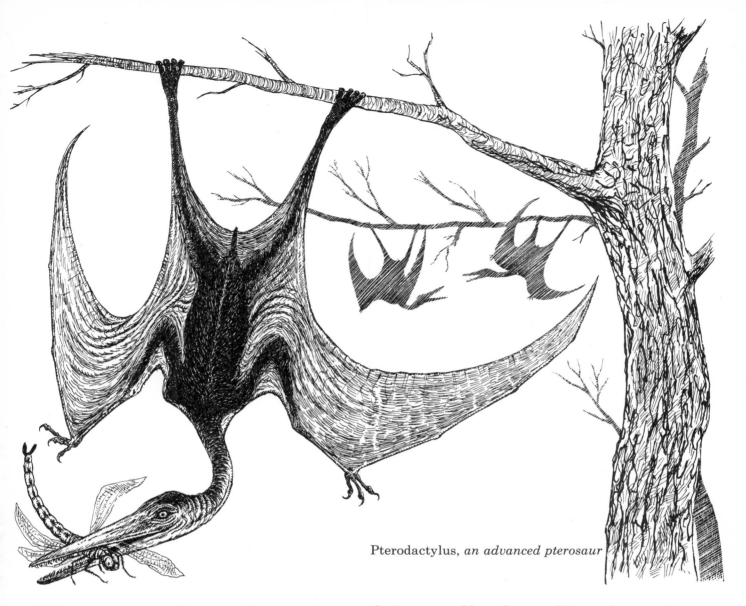

Pterodactylus, *an advanced pterosaur*

What was an advanced pterosaur like?

A more advanced form of pterosaur had much broader wings and a short tail. A typical member of this group was *Pterodactylus*. This was about the same size as *Rhamphorhynchus* and lived at the same time and in the same area in southern Germany. We know what this pterosaur looked like because, like *Rhamphorhynchus*, it was fossilized in fine limestone.

Palaeontologists used to think that the pterosaurs were gliders rather than flyers. We now think that they were more likely to have been flyers. By spreading their arms and legs they could have stretched their wings to their greatest area and would have been able to produce a powerful downstroke. By folding their arms and legs they could have decreased the area of the wing for a quick upstroke before the next strong downstroke.

For all this activity, and for the brain power needed to control it, the pterosaurs must have been warm-blooded – just like today's birds. Proof of this came in 1971 when a pterosaur skeleton that had fossilized hair attached to it was found in the Soviet Union. The hair would have kept the body warm and helped to control the heat flow.

What is a pterodactyl?

You will often hear people talk about 'pterodactyls'. This is a popular and useful name for any animal that belonged to the pterosaur group. The name 'pterodactyl' means 'winged finger'.

129

Dsungaripterus, *an advanced pterosaur with no teeth in the front of the jaws*

How did pterosaurs develop?

As we have seen, both primitive and advanced pterosaurs lived during the Jurassic period. The primitive had narrow wings and a tail, while the advanced had broad wings and no tail. Why was one type more advanced than the other?

The tail developed in primitive pterosaurs to balance the animal while flying, but this made it slow to manoeuvre. The advanced types lost the tail and had to keep their balance by controlling their wings. The brain grew bigger to manage all this. At the same time the heavy teeth of the pterosaurs were replaced by a light toothless beak.

The pterosaur's body was beautifully designed for flight. The bones were hollow to keep down weight, as in modern birds. The backbone at the shoulders was fused into a stiff, strong lump and the shoulders fixed firmly to it to support the wings.

Pteranodon, *the toothless fishing pterosaur of the Upper Cretaceous*

Quetzalcoatlus, *probably the biggest flying creature that ever lived*

What were Cretaceous pterosaurs like?

The pterosaurs existed right up until the end of the age of dinosaurs. In the Upper Cretaceous they became very advanced creatures indeed.

Pteranodon of the Upper Cretaceous of Kansas used to be regarded as the biggest flying animal that ever lived. It was one of the advanced forms of pterosaur, with no tail. It had a strange hammer-shaped head with a long toothless beak sticking out at the front and a long bony crest sticking out at the back. We are sure that it ate fish, and it must have scooped them from the sea while slowly flying low over the waves. The crest may have balanced the head while it speared the fish. It could not have landed on the water because it could never have taken off again. It probably roosted on rocky islands and looked after its young, just as gannets and other seabirds do today.

Which was the biggest pterosaur?

We used to think that *Pteranodon*, with a wingspan of 8 metres (26 feet), was the biggest of the pterosaurs. Then, in 1971, bones of a truly enormous pterosaur were found in Upper Cretaceous rocks in Texas. We still do not know a great deal about it, except that it had a long neck and a wingspan that must have reached 12 metres (39 feet). Its weight was about 80 kg (180 lb) – five times the weight of the biggest of today's flying birds. It must have been as big as any flying creature could possibly be – but that is what we used to say about *Pteranodon*! Unlike *Pteranodon* this creature flew over inland plains. It was probably a scavenger, feeding on the bodies of dead dinosaurs and living rather as the big vultures do today. The scientific name of this monster is *Quetzalcoatlus*. It is named after an ancient Mexican god that took the form of a flying serpent.

131

Archaeopteryx, *the first bird, chased by the coelurosaur* Compsognathus

What was the relationship between these two creatures? (See page 50)

When did birds develop?

The Upper Jurassic was the heyday of the pterosaurs, but it also saw the evolution of the birds. *Archaeopteryx* of southern Germany is the best-known of the early birds, although palaeontologists have found a fossil feather in earlier Jurassic rocks of North America. *Archaeopteryx* must be very close to the ancestor of the birds because its skeleton is half dinosaur (see page 50).

A bird's wing is totally different from that of a pterosaur (see page 128). The expanse of feathers is more efficient and less vulnerable than a single flap of skin. A bird's wing, being more efficient, could be smaller than a pterosaur's wing. Birds and pterosaurs probably lived in the same area but not competing with one another. The pterosaurs may have flown in the open skies, while the birds stayed in the forests and fluttered in the undergrowth.

Hesperornis, *the flightless sea-bird from the Upper Cretaceous of Kansas*

What were Cretaceous birds like?

By Upper Cretaceous times the bird groups that we know today had evolved. Owls, terns, cormorants and waders shared the landscape with the dinosaurs. These were true birds – unlike the half-dinosaur *Archaeopteryx*. They had proper bird-like tails, and beaks instead of heavy toothed jaws.

However, there were also some very strange specialized birds. Already some were losing their powers of flight and taking to a ground-dwelling or a swimming existence. *Hesperornis* was one of these. It looked a bit like a penguin, almost 2 metres (6.5 feet) high, but without any trace of wings. It was a sea bird and was extremely well adapted to a sea-dwelling lifestyle. It spent most of its time in the water, swimming with its webbed feet and catching fish with its beak – a beak that still retained teeth.

133

What lived in the Mesozoic seas?

We are more likely to find fossils of animals that lived in the water than those that lived on land. This means we know much more about sea creatures living during the age of dinosaurs than we do about the dinosaurs themselves. There were no sea-living dinosaurs, as far as we know, but many other types of reptile lived in the sea during that time.

Life evolved in the sea and later came out on to the land. There is always food to eat in the sea, so it is not surprising that many animals left the land and went back to their ancestral home. Nowadays, mammals such as the whales and seals have done this. In the Mesozoic it was the reptiles.

What would an animal eat in the sea?

The sea is full of food. Tiny microscopic plants and animals live in the surface waters. These are eaten by little fish which are eaten by larger fish. There are all sorts of sea creatures, such as shrimps, shellfish and squid, as well as seaweed which grows everywhere. If a large animal leaves the land to live in the sea, it could eat any of these sea creatures and plants but usually an animal that has returned to the sea eats fish.

The Mesozoic saw the spread of broad continental shelves and shallow seas. New marine invertebrates (animals without a backbone) evolved, including the ammonites – squid-like creatures with coiled shells. These were also taken as food by the great sea reptiles of the time.

The chalk seas of Upper Cretaceous Kansas were inhabited by huge sea reptiles such as the 9 m (30 ft) seagoing lizard Tylosaurus *and the long-necked plesiosaur* Elasmosaurus. *There were also several specialized sea-birds*

How would a land animal change for sea-life?

We know that any animal living in a particular environment will take on the right kind of shape to live in that environment (see page 21).

The sea shows this beautifully. An animal that lives in the sea must have a streamlined shape so it can slip through the water without much effort. It must have something to push it along through the water. Usually this is a set of paddles that can thrust backwards against the water, or a flat-finned tail that can push against the water as it is waved from side to side. It must have the right kind of teeth for its food, and in the sea this usually means a large number of fine pointed teeth for catching and holding slippery fish.

Less obvious, but just as important, is the ability to live at great depths beneath the surface. No animal that has returned to the sea has ever redeveloped gills to extract oxygen from the water. A sea-living reptile still has to breathe air and has to come to the surface at frequent intervals. Animals that are quite at home in the sea, such as whales, can take a breath that will last them for an hour or more.

At great depths the pressure on an animal's body will be far greater than at the surface. A sea animal must have a blood system that will still circulate under these conditions. Some reptiles developed special bony strengthening in the eyes so that they could still focus under pressure.

There is also the problem of giving birth in the water. The reptile egg would be no good for this. We shall see how different reptiles solved this in different ways.

Elasmosaurus

Hesperornis

Proganochelys, *the 70 cm (28 in) long turtle ancestor from the Triassic*

Turtle plates are easily fossilized

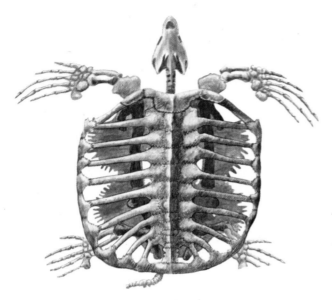

Archelon, *the greatest turtle that ever lived*

Which was the most successful sea reptile

The most successful, from the fact that it is still around today, must be the turtle.

The first of the group that we know about is *Proganochelys* from the Middle Triassic of Germany. This land-dwelling creature had an unmistakable turtle-like shell. It was very primitive in that it had teeth and ribs. No other turtles have these – the teeth are replaced by horny ridges in the mouth and the ribs are unnecesary because of the support given by the shell.

Many later members of the group took to living in the sea so that the water could support the weight of the shell. They have changed very little to this day.

The shell was a great defence mechanism, and soon the shoulder and hip bones were embedded inside it and the legs could be protected. In the early types there was no way

of protecting the head, but by the Cretaceous the head could be pulled into the shell as well. This could be done either by pulling the neck in sideways or by pulling the head straight back. Two distinct lines of turtles developed, based on this difference, and we still have them both today.

The limbs of the seagoing turtles developed into paddles. In cross-section the paddle was rather like the wing of a bird. The turtle moved through the water with a flying action.

We know quite a bit about the turtles of the past. Their shells fossilize quite easily – more easily than the bones of other vertebrates. The largest turtle that we know was *Archelon* from the Upper Cretaceous of Kansas. It was about 4 metres (13 feet) long.

What other early Mesozoic sea reptiles were there?

The Triassic turtles had distant relatives that lived in the same seas. These were the placodonts. In appearance they looked like huge newts, 2 metres (6.5 feet) long. Their

bodies were quite stout and had bony armour plates set into the skin on the back. The tail was long and would have been used for swimming. The legs had not changed much from a typical land-reptile's legs. There seems to have been a ridge down the back, that merged into a swimming fin along the top surface of the tail.

We can see from the teeth that placodonts ate shellfish. They used their protruding front teeth to prise the shellfish from their rocks and the huge flat teeth on the palate for crushing the shells. The placodonts died out at the end of the Triassic.

A Triassic reptilian oddity was *Tanystropheus*. This was related to the lizards and was about 4 metres (13 feet) long. However 3 metres (10 feet) of this was neck! The neck bones were so long that they were at first thought to be leg bones! It probably lived by the seashore and dipped its neck into rock pools in search of shellfish.

A group of reptiles that were well placed to take up a seagoing life were the crocodiles. They spent much of their time in water and during the Jurassic a group of truly marine crocodiles developed. These had long sinuous bodies, paddles for legs and a fish-like fin on the end of the tail. Unlike their land-living relatives these sea crocodiles had no bony plates embedded in their skin. Their outer surface was smooth and streamlined. These were the geosaurs, and they chased fish in the shallow seas of the Upper Jurassic.

Skull of Placodus, *showing the powerful teeth it needed for dealing with shellfish*

Placodus, *the shellfish-eater of the Tethys Sea*

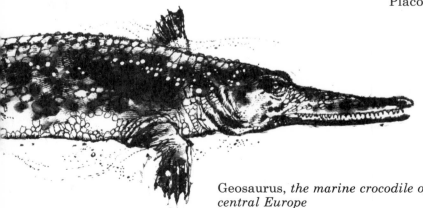

Geosaurus, *the marine crocodile of Jurassic central Europe*

Nothosaurus, *one of the ancestors of the*
plesiosaurs

What was a plesiosaur?

When we think of sea reptiles we often think
of sea serpents – imaginary sea monsters that
terrified our sailor ancestors. The Mesozoic
saw a group of swimming animals that closely
resembled these fictitious creatures. They
were the plesiosaurs.

The plesiosaurs evolved in the Triassic from
a group of aquatic reptiles. These earlier
creatures, called nothosaurs, had a lizard-like
body, long neck and very long snaggle-
toothed jaws. They lived on the rocks and
beaches that bordered the Tethys Sea catching fish. Their feet were webbed, and they had
a fin along the tail. Nothosaurs were usually
less than 1 metre (3 feet) long but some
reached lengths of 3 metres (10 feet) or more.
This widespread group of animals ranged from
southern Europe and north Africa to China.

The plesiosaurs evolved directly from them
as the heads became smaller, the necks longer
and thinner, the bodies broader and flatter,
and the limbs transformed into powerful
paddles.

Plesiosaur paddle showing the elongated toes

A shoal of Cryptocleidus, *a 2 m (6.5 ft) plesiosaur*
from the Middle Jurassic of England

How did they develop?

Once they had evolved the plesiosaurs divided into two lines. The most typical was the elasmosaur line. These were the long-necked plesiosaurs with the small heads. They lasted to the very end of the Cretaceous and produced *Elasmosaurus* – a huge creature 10 metres (33 feet) long with a neck that contained 76 vertebrae.

The second line was that of the pliosaurs – the short-necked plesiosaurs. These were the whales of the Mesozoic seas. They had huge heads, short necks and barrel-shaped bodies. They probably cruised the Jurassic and Cretaceous seas eating big ammonites and squid. They were not as common as the elasmosaurs. The biggest was probably *Kronosaurus*, from the Lower Cretaceous of Australia. It was 13 metres (43 feet) long and had a head that reached a length of 2.7 metres.

Kronosaurus, *the largest pliosaur*

Elasmosaurus, *the longest elasmosaur*

How did plesiosaurs live?

Imagine a snake threaded through the body of a turtle. That is how the 19th century palaeontologist William Buckland described a plesiosaur. He was not far wrong. A typical plesiosaur body, although it did not have a shell, was broad and flat, and very much like that of a turtle. The paddles were very turtle-like. The neck was long and snaky and with the small head on the end it must have looked just like a snake.

How would such a creature have lived? We can tell from the teeth that it must have eaten fish. The body is that of a slow-moving creature, so it probably did most of its hunting by dashing out its head and neck and snapping at the fish before they had a chance to swim away. We have found plesiosaur skeletons with piles of stones where the stomach would have been. These were probably swallowed by the animal to help it to grind up the food in its stomach. Certain birds, such as swans, do this today, and we think that some of the dinosaurs may have done so as well.

The paddles were long and tapering. Their toes were fused together to form them, and each toe had more than the usual number of bones. Palaeontologists used to think that the paddles worked by pushing against the water but now they think it more likely that they were moved in a figure-of-eight pattern, enabling the plesiosaur to fly through the water in the same way as a turtle does.

Plesiosaurs could not have laid eggs in the water. They probably came ashore to bury their eggs on a beach – like a turtle.

139

Which was the most fish-like sea reptile?

Ichthyosaurus means 'fish lizard' and this aptly describes a creature that lived in the Jurassic seas. It looked like a kind of shark or dolphin. It had a perfectly streamlined shape, from its pointed snout, past its narrow head which joined the bulbous body without any visible neck, down to a fish-like tail. It had two pairs of paddles – the larger pair at the front – and a triangular fin on the back. There were many types of ichthyosaur but they all had this similar shape – and they were all reptiles.

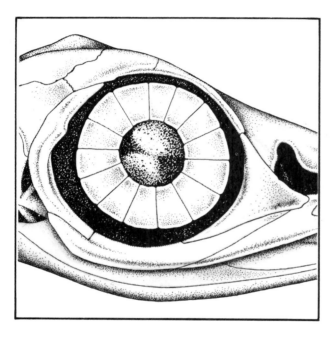

An ichthyosaur's eye had a ring of bone to support it against the pressure of the water

How do we know?

A little girl of 11 – Mary Anning – found the first ichthyosaur skeleton in Lower Jurassic rocks of southern England in 1810. Later palaeontologists restored it as simply a swimming lizard. When other fossils came to light they wondered why they all seemed to have broken tails. When complete ichthyosaur skeletons were found preserved in shales in southern Germany palaeontologists had a better idea of what the animal looked like. In the German finds, the soft parts of the body were preserved as a thin film of carbon in the body's shape. They could see the fin on the back and the fish-tail that was supported by the down-turned backbone. From the cells left behind they could even tell that the ichthyosaurs had been a brown tortoiseshell colour.

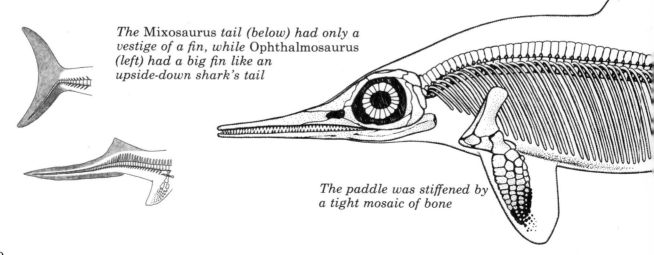

The Mixosaurus *tail (below) had only a vestige of a fin, while* Ophthalmosaurus *(left) had a big fin like an upside-down shark's tail*

The paddle was stiffened by a tight mosaic of bone

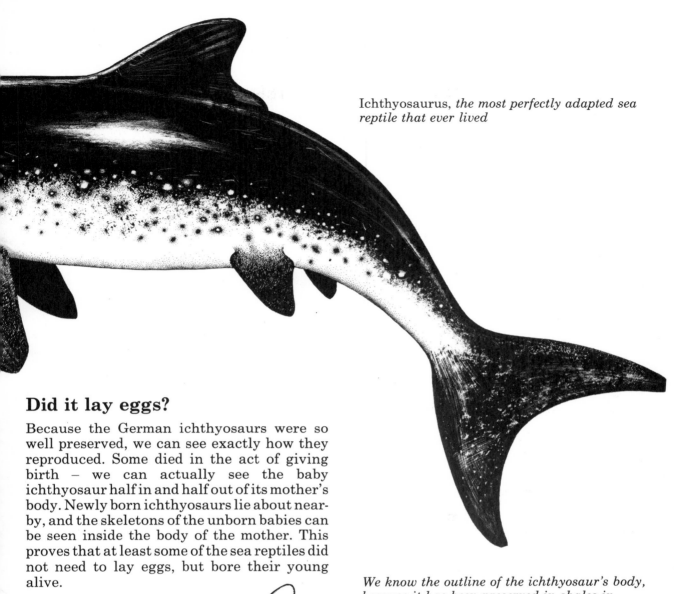

Ichthyosaurus, *the most perfectly adapted sea reptile that ever lived*

Did it lay eggs?

Because the German ichthyosaurs were so well preserved, we can see exactly how they reproduced. Some died in the act of giving birth – we can actually see the baby ichthyosaur half in and half out of its mother's body. Newly born ichthyosaurs lie about nearby, and the skeletons of the unborn babies can be seen inside the body of the mother. This proves that at least some of the sea reptiles did not need to lay eggs, but bore their young alive.

We know the outline of the ichthyosaur's body, because it has been preserved in shales in southern Germany

The bend in the tail puzzled early palaeontologists

How many were there?

We know there were many different kinds of ichthyosaurs. The earliest was Triassic *Mixosaurus* which was long and thin with hardly a trace of a fish-tail. The largest, *Ophthalmosaurus*, was 3 metres (10 feet) long and had a toothless beak. *Eurhinosaurus* was rather like a swordfish, with the upper jaw far longer than the lower.

The ichthyosaurs were very successful for their time, but died out early in the Cretaceous. They were replaced by the mosasaurs, such as *Tylosaurus*, as the big fish-eaters of the time.

What killed the dinosaurs?

About 65 million years ago the dinosaurs died out. With them perished the pterosaurs, the great sea-living reptiles, and many, many of the smaller invertebrates that had existed throughout the Mesozoic. Not one of these creatures survives today. We do not know why this happened, or what caused it, although many palaeontologists have their own theories.

Whatever happened must have affected both the continents and the oceans. Yet the event was selective. Not everything was wiped out. Why, for example, were the dinosaurs killed and not the crocodiles? Why were the pterosaurs exterminated and not the birds? Why were the mosasaurs wiped out and not the sharks?

Any theory that is put forward to account for the catastrophic extinctions at the end of the Cretaceous period must account for the survivals as well.

Was it a sudden event?

Early palaeontologists could see that the animal life of the Earth had changed from time to time. The Cretaceous mass extinction was not the only one. They thought that this must have been due to catastrophies, such as worldwide earthquakes or all-engulfing floods. Once palaeontology and geology became established as recognized sciences these ideas fell into disfavour. Nowadays they are back.

Palaeontologists have found traces of the element irridium in the beds at the very top of the Cretaceous. This element is usually only found in meteorites. They think that a giant meteorite, the size of a city, must have hit the earth at this time and sent up clouds of dust and steam. These clouds would have cut off the sun and plunged the earth into darkness for a few years. Plants would have died off and so would the animals that fed on them. Plants can grow again from seed after a long time. Animals can't.

Was the extinction of the dinosaurs a gradual process?

The theories of 'catastrophism' in which the dinosaurs, and the other creatures, were wiped out suddenly by some dramatic event are very attractive. The dust-cloud thrown up by a meteorite would have killed off the big animals on the land, but it should not have affected the smaller animals in the sea. Another catastrophic theory is that a cloud of dust passed through the solar system at this time and cut down the light from the sun, with the same result. Or an exploding star could have drenched the earth in deadly radiation that the dinosaurs could not have survived. Many palaeontologists disagree with these ideas.

They say that the extinctions were really quite gradual processes. A million years is a very short time in geological terms – hardly noticeable in the thickness of rocks formed during that time – but in evolutionary terms it can be quite a while.

It seems that the climate changed at the end of the Cretaceous period. We can see this by the change in vegetation. The change was probably due to the fact that, as the continents drifted apart, there were fewer broad shallow seas. The smaller water area meant that less carbon dioxide gas could be dissolved in it. This in turn meant that there was more carbon dioxide in the atmosphere, giving warmer climates.

Dinosaurs, being enormous, heavy reptiles, could not have withstood the increase in temperature and would have perished. Because less oxygen was dissolved in the sea, fewer marine plants could exist, affecting other sea life as well.

These effects would not have harmed small land-living animals, especially if they were warm-blooded and so could withstand changes in temperature. Hence the mammals and birds survived. In the sea the less specialized creatures, like sharks that had existed happily in all sorts of conditions for millennia, would have been unperturbed by the changes and would also have survived.

What followed the dinosaurs?

A mass extinction always produces a spurt of evolution. If one group of animals dies out it leaves a food supply that can be eaten by something else. With the dinosaurs out of the way the mammals could develop to take their place.

Ever since the Triassic period when they first appeared the mammals had been small, insignificant creatures, scurrying and dodging about between the feet of the dinosaurs. They had not developed into larger animals because all the available lifestyles were occupied by the reptiles. But now they could really be something!

The Cenozoic – the period that started about 65 million years ago and did not finish until about two million years ago – was the age of mammals. The early part of it showed a sudden flourishing of mammal types. And what incredible mammal types they were! It was as if nature were trying out all sorts of different shapes and styles to see which would survive best.

Mammals were able to grow bigger, which they could not do while the dinosaurs were around. Rhinoceros-shapes and hippopotamus-shapes developed. There were mammals that climbed trees, mammals that lived in rivers, mammals that ate mammals. Flying mammals – the bats – developed once the pterosaurs had gone. Sea mammals – the whales – evolved in the absence of plesiosaurs.

Uintatherium, *a rhinoceros-like Lower Cenozoic mammal*

Coryphodon, *a hippopotamus-like form*

Phenacodus, *the ancestor of the running mammals*

A pantothere, one of the primitive shrew-like mammals from the age of dinosaurs

How many mammal types?

During the age of dinosaurs there were several groups of mammals in existence, all quite different from one another. Not all of these survived into the Cenozoic. Three that did became the mammals that we know today.

The first were the monotremes. These were very primitive and still laid eggs. Only two survive today – the duckbilled platypus and the spiny echidna, both from Australia.

The second group were the marsupials. These gave birth to their young at a very early stage and nursed them in a pouch. We still have plenty of marsupials today, but they nearly all live in Australia.

The third group were the placentals – and these were the ones that were most successful. They gave birth to their young at a very advanced stage – a foal can run as soon as it is born. Most of today's mammals, including ourselves, are placentals.

What were Cenozoic birds like?

As with the mammals, all the bird types that we have today were in existence during the Lower Cenozoic. There were a number of odd-looking types as well, however.

In some places, before carnivorous mammals had evolved, the birds became the predatory hunters. These fierce birds were flightless and looked so much like the old carnosaurs that it seemed as if nature had regretted killing off the meat-eating dinosaurs!

Diatryma from the Lower Cenozoic of North America and Europe stood about 2 metres (6.5 feet) high. It had powerful legs built for running and a wicked beak that would have made short work of any small mammal.

Phororhacos of South America was a similar size. This lived somewhat later but South America was an island continent at the time and meat-eating mammals did not evolve there until much later.

Phororhacos

Diatryma

What was the Lower Cenozoic environment?

The climate over most of the world was warm and humid. Lush forests and woodlands covered many areas. Nearly all the varied mammal and bird life was adapted for forest existence.

The Lower Cenozoic forests of southern England

147

What was the Upper Cenozoic like?

A great change took place to the landscape of the Upper Cenozoic, and this was due to the fact that grass evolved. Grasslands spread where there once was forest and these grasslands could support all kinds of new mammals. At the same time the movements of the continents was throwing up the great mountain ranges of today – the Alps, the Himalayas and the Andes. We could almost have recognized the Upper Cenozoic world.

What kinds of animals lived on the grasslands?

The important thing about grass is that the leaves grow from the base, not from the tips. This means that if the top is damaged, it keeps on growing. An animal can eat grass right down to ground level and it will grow back up again. With the spread of such grasslands, new types of mammals evolved. We call these mammals 'grazers'.

A grazer must have very special teeth. Grass is full of the chemical silica which is the same material that glass is made of. The teeth of an ordinary animal would be worn away in no time, so grazers have very hard teeth, with strong grinding surfaces.

The grasslands are wide open spaces – any meat-eating animal can be seen coming from a long way away. Grazers usually have long legs, so they can run away when they see a predator coming. Because of their long legs the body is held very high above the ground. The neck then also has to be long so that the head can reach down for the grass. Often the head is long as well, to keep the eyes above the grass level while the animal is eating. All grazers have these features.

The horse is a typical grazer. However, it evolved from a tiny rabbit-sized animal that browsed in Lower Cenozoic forests. Fossils in North America show us just how the horse evolved into today's magnificent running animal.

The design of the horse was so good that it evolved elsewhere. *Thoatherium* lived on the Upper Cenozoic grasslands of the South American island continent. It looked like a small horse but was not related.

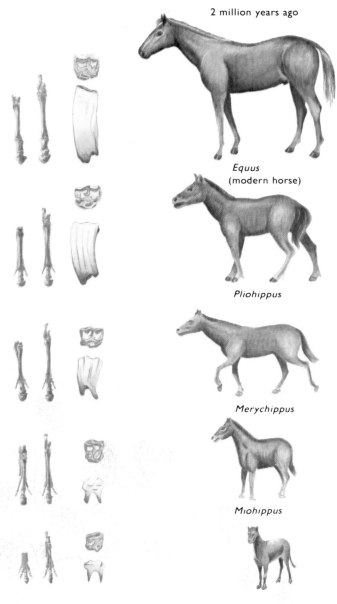

2 million years ago

Equus
(modern horse)

Pliohippus

Merychippus

Miohippus

50 million years ago *Hyracotherium*

As the horse developed from Hyracotherium *to* Equus *the toes (far left) were reduced to one, and the teeth became higher and more wrinkled*

Thoatherium, *the horse-like South American grazer*

Baluchitherium, *the tallest mamal that ever lived*

Moropus, *the clawed horse*

What other mammals were there?

The Lower Cenozoic experimented with all sorts of fantastic mammal types. In the Upper Cenozoic the strangest of these were weeded out. Most of those that survived were quite similar to those that we have today.

Would we recognize the Upper Cenozoic mammals?

Although all of today's mammal groups were present during the Upper Cenozoic, not many of them looked very much like the animals we see in a modern zoo.

We have seen how the horse developed into today's form. There were other relatives of the horse that were quite different. *Moropus* looked quite like a horse, but it had no hooves. Instead it had clawed toes, probably for digging up roots.

The rhinoceroses were around as well, but there were all sorts of different kinds. There were, indeed, the large stocky horned types that we have today, but there were also lightly-built types. Living on the grasslands were herds of running rhinoceros that looked a little like the early horses. The biggest land mammal that ever lived was a kind of rhinoceros. *Baluchitherium* was a rhinoceros that stood 6 metres (20 feet) high at the shoulder. It must have browsed from treetops in central Asia where it lived.

Elephants, deer and mice had all evolved by this time, as had the cats and dogs and their relatives that hunted them.

An Upper Cenozoic landscape, showing open woodland and grassland

What was the Ice Age?

At the end of the Cenozoic, about 2 million years ago, the climate began to cool. Temperatures worldwide dropped until the ice caps at the North and South Poles began to expand and creep down into lower latitudes. They did not cover the whole Earth but most of Europe, Asia and North America were enveloped in a blanket of ice and snow. In the rest of the world, the tropical forests and deserts that we have today were still there, but they were all crammed together along the equator.

Snow piled up in mountain valleys, became compressed and turned into ice. Glaciers moved down from the mountains, merged and spread over the lowlands as ice sheets. They ground out new valleys as they went and carried rocks and debris for many miles. Cold, treeless plains (tundra) stretched out around the glaciers' margins. The ground here was marshy with a frozen sub-soil so the only vegetation was mosses, lichens and low-growing bushes.

What were Ice Age animals like?

The harsh conditions acted as yet another spur to evolution. Mammals developed that were particularly well adapted to the cold conditions. The large animals of the time grew shaggy coats and were able to live off the sparser vegetation. The woolly mammoth and the woolly rhinoceros of Europe and the mastodon of North America were typical.

The mammoth, as well as its shaggy coat, had a hump of fat on its shoulders to feed it when conditions were particularly bad. Its long curving tusks were used to shovel away snow from the mosses and lichens on which it fed. We know a great deal about mammoths because we have found their bodies perfectly preserved where they have fallen into muddy bogs and frozen.

It is unlikely that the mammoths, the woolly rhinoceroses and the other animals of the time would be able to survive amongst the ice and tundra of the far north today. However, during the Ice Age, the glaciers and the tundra were much further south, and were surrounded by much more vegetation. This was mostly birch and coniferous forest, and many different animals could live amongst it.

What significant creature evolved in the Ice Age?

The Ice Age saw the development of a group of creatures that were to have a greater impact on the earth than any other that had ever existed – man.

Our scientific name is *Homo sapiens*, and the first species of *Homo* probably evolved from an ape-like creature called *Australopithecus* at the beginning of the Ice Age. *Homo habilis* or 'handy man' was the first toolmaker and evolved in Africa. From this developed *Homo erectus* or 'upright man' and he spread across the globe from Africa to Europe and China. His great discovery was the use of fire. Our own species, *Homo sapiens* or 'thinking man', evolved about a million years ago in Europe and from him developed all the great civilizations of today.

Ice Age scene in northern Europe showing horses, reindeer, mammoth, woolly rhinoceros, musk ox and wolf

Homo habilis, *the first creature to make and use tools*

The maximum extent of the ice sheets during the Ice Age

Was the Ice Age cold all the time?

The Ice Age was not one long continuous cold spell. What happened was that the ice sheets came and went several times. What we actually regard as the Ice Age was just the conditions during glacial advance, when the ice reached down across northern Europe, Asia and North America. Between these advances were periods that we call 'interglacials' in which the climate was even warmer than it is now.

These interglacials lasted tens of thousands of years. During them northern Europe looked quite subtropical. Elephants, lions and rhinoceroses roamed the banks of the River Thames where London now stands.

Is it all over?

You may have noticed how the weather is not the same from one year to the next. The climate seems to be changing all the time. In fact, it is only about ten thousand years since the last glacial advance. It may well be that we are just in another interglacial and that at some time in the future the glaciers and tundra of the Ice Age will return.

Interglacial scene in northern Europe, showing elephants, rhinoceros, deer, lion and hyena

Who were the great palaeontologists?

All our knowledge of past life has come from the work of a very large number of palaeontologists. In the history of palaeontology there are a few people who are particularly famous for one reason or another. Most of them went out and discovered fossils, but some were theoreticians who worked on specimens found by other people and developed ideas around them.

Mary Anning

Baron Georges Cuvier

Who invented palaeontology?

Baron Georges Cuvier (1769–1832), a French geologist and zoologist, studied modern animals and then applied the same study to fossils, giving birth to the science. He believed that life changed in the past through a series of catastrophies.

Were there famous amateur palaeontologists?

Mary Anning (1799–1847) lived in Lyme Regis in southern England. She collected fossils and started selling them when she was 10 years old. She found the entire skeleton of *Ichthyosaurus* in 1810.

Who worked out the ideas of evolution?

Many people throughout history had the idea that organisms changed as time went on, but perhaps the most famous person who developed this idea was Charles Robert Darwin (1809–82). He was a British naturalist who sailed on a scientific expedition on HMS *Beagle* between 1831 and 1836 to the Atlantic, South America and the Pacific. What he saw of island life and of South American fossils led him to write a series of books explaining evolution. He proposed the idea of natural selection, or the survival of the fittest, to account for evolutionary changes. He collaborated in this with another zoologist, Alfred Russell Wallace (1823–1913).

Darwin's ideas were disliked by the established church of the day. His friend, Thomas Huxley, argued publicly on his behalf, leading to the widespread acceptance of his ideas at the time.

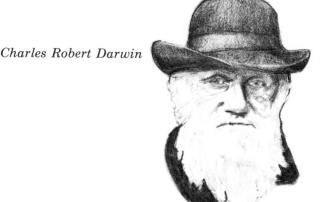

Charles Robert Darwin

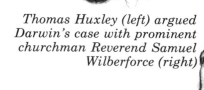

Thomas Huxley (left) argued Darwin's case with prominent churchman Reverend Samuel Wilberforce (right)

Doctor Gideon Algernon Mantell

Dean William Buckland

Sir Richard Owen

Who first discovered dinosaurs?

William Buckland (1784–1856), a British geologist and theologian, was a great follower of Cuvier's ideas of catastrophism. He was the first to discover a dinosaur and recognize it as a huge reptile. This was *Megalosaurus*, which means 'big lizard', and he found it near Oxford in 1824.

Gideon Algernon Mantell (1790–1852) found the second dinosaur to be described. This was *Iguanodon* which he discovered in south-east England. Its name means 'iguana toothed' and he recognized it as being a big reptile, although his restorations were inaccurate (see page 18).

Who were the American dinosaur hunters?

Othniel Charles Marsh (1831–99) and Edward Drinker Cope (1840–97) were two of the most famous fossil hunters that ever lived. They were great rivals and each spent years trying to better the achievements of the other. They both worked in the Morrison Formation and elsewhere in North America, fighting each other and hostile Indians. Amongst other things, Marsh discovered *Diplodocus*, *Allosaurus*, *Stegosaurus* and *Triceratops*, while Cope found *Camarasaurus*, *Monoclonius* and *Coelophysis*.

Who invented the name 'dinosaur'?

Sir Richard Owen (1804–92), a British doctor and palaeontologist suggested the scientific name *Dinosauria*, 'terrible lizard', in 1841, after the finds of Buckland and Mantell.

Othniel Charles Marsh

Edward Drinker Cope

INDEX

Figures in italics refer to illustrations only

of *Archaeopteryx* 50
of *Ichthyosaurus* 140–1
of *Iguanadon* 83
of *Psittacosaurus* 88
of *Stegosaurus* 113, *115*
skin 16, 18, 85, 93, 94, 113, 118, 119,
    121, 127, 128, 133, 137
  fossilized *94*
skull, 18, 21, 30, 57, 59, 66, 71, 72, 73,
    82, 86, 89, 91, 93, 98, 107, 108,
    112, 115, 118–9, 121
  Brachylophosaurus 95
  Camarasaurus 73
  Diadectes 21
  Diplodocus 72
  Heterodontosaurus 82
  Iguanodon 82
  Ornithomimus 51
  Parasaurolophus 93
  Placodus 137
  Proceratops 98
  prosauropod *68*
  sabre-toothed tiger *21*
  Saurolophus 93
  Stegosaurus 115
  Triceratops 107
snakes 37, 139
spiders 33
spikes 46, 85, 92, 105, 117, 119, 122
spines 55, 62, 66, 87, 111, 112, 113, 118,
    121, 124, 127
Spinosaurus 55, *58*, 59, 87, 113
  aegypticus 62
Spriggina 25
stance 42, 43, 46, 121
stegosaurs 46, 47, *110*, 111–5, 117, 118,
    124
  family tree *111*
Stegosaurus 111, 112, 153
Stereocephalus 124
stipe 29
stones 78, 139
Strophomena 27
Struthiosaurus 117, 123
Styracosaurus 97, *104*, 105
sucker 30
'Supersaurus' 76
swamp 20, 33, 34, 38, *39*, 56, 72, 112
Syringopora 28

T

tar 12
Tarbosaurus 61, 62
teeth 19, 21, 35, 56, 62, 66, 72, 73, 81,
    82, 85, 86, 91, 98, 101, 103, 112,
    124, 130, 135, 136, 137, 148
  Coelophysis 49
  hadrosaur *91*
  horse *148*
  Placodus 137
  prosauropod *68*
  shark 12
temperature 35, 45, 59, 87, 113
Teratosaurus 55, 62
Tethys Sea 37, 138
Tetragraptus 29
thecodonts 34, 35, 42, 46, 47, 48, *54*, 55,
    68, 118
theropods 48–63, 65, 68, 82, 112, 113
Thoatherium 148

tiger, sabre-toothed 21
time 10, 24, 25
Titanosaurus 65
toads 32
toes 60, 68, 81, 82, 85, 91, 99, *138*
tools 15
Torosaurus 97
trace fossil 13, 78
trees 20, 33, 37, 103
  family 48, 55, 65, 81, 90, 97, 107, 111,
    117
Triassic period 10, 13, 26, 35, 46, 48,
    62, 65, 68, 81, 127, 136, 137, 146
  landscape *36*
  world map *37*
Triceratops 96, *97*, 106, *107*, *109*, 153
  brevicornis 107
  family tree *107*
  flabellatus 107
  horridus 106, 107
  serratus 107
trilobite *26*, 27
Tsintaosaurus 90, 93
tuatara 34
Tuojiangosaurus *111*, 114
turtle 136, 139
Tylosaurus 21, *134*, 141
Tyrannosaurus 43, 52, *55*, 62, *108–9*
  rex 62, *63*

U

Uintatherium 146
'Ultrasaurus' 76, *76–7*

V

Velociraptor 48, 101
vertebrae 17, 66, 72, 76, 122
vertebrate 17, 30, 31
volcanoes 24

W

Wallace, Alfred 152
weapons 122
whale *21*, 134, 139, 146
wings 127, 128, 129, 130, 133, 136
  comparison of *128*
wolf 150
wood, petrified 13
woodlice 27
worms 25, 26, 30